# GRASS
# LEFT
# STANDING

# GRASS LEFT STANDING

## A Park Interpreter's Roadmap to Forest Bathing

# MAUREEN STINE

MISSION POINT PRESS

Readers are encouraged to go to www.MissionPointPress.com to contact the author or to find information on how to buy this book in bulk at a discounted rate.

MISSION POINT PRESS

Published by Mission Point Press
2554 Chandler Rd.
Traverse City, MI 49696
(231) 421-9513
www.MissionPointPress.com

Print ISBN: 978-1-961302-40-2
Library of Congress Control Number: 2024903919

Printed in the United States of America

*For Aunt Mo,*
*Our family's original forest bather. You showed us kids how to lay in*
*the grass and gaze up at the clouds and daydream when it was a really*
*important time in our lives to learn to do that. We never forgot.*


*For Dave and your sweet accompaniment on all our forest saunters*
*together.*


*For Tim, Madelynn, Anastasia, Timmy, Steve, Meg, Andrea, Heather,*
*Josh, Kevin, Luke, Billy², Mickey, Tommy, Teddy…and Truman.*

*Interpretation is a mission-based communication process that forges emotional and intellectual connections between the interests of the audience and meanings inherent in the resource.*
—National Association for Interpretation (2006 Definitions Project)


*Forest Therapy, also known as Forest Bathing, is a relational practice that brings people into deeper intimacy with natural places.*
—Association of Nature and Forest Therapy Guides and Programs


*Grass left standing is an agricultural term describing fallow or unplanted cropland acres which are part of a rotation, where cultivated land that is normally planted is purposely kept out of production during a regular growing season. Resting the ground in this manner allows it to recover its fertility and conserve moisture for crop production in the next growing season.*
—United States Department of Agriculture, Farm Service Agency

# CONTENTS

# FOREWORD

Forest bathing! An initial encounter with the concept might evoke different, perhaps comical, mental images in the minds of readers unacquainted with its meaning. However, for me it resonated deeply and immediately transported me to the very origins of my relationship with the natural world, shaping the course of my life's journey. This journey, both personal and professional, has led me to appreciate the profound impact of nature on our well-being, and it is this appreciation that Maureen Stine so beautifully explores in the following pages.

I remember it vividly, as if it were yesterday. I was just seven years old on a family vacation, snugly wrapped in the warmth of a cabin bed when my mother gently roused me from my sleep. "Get dressed and follow me outside," she whispered. Full of curiosity and interest I complied. Stepping out into the cool misty spring morning, I found myself in a scene straight out of a postcard-perfect world—an ancient pine forest that framed a small, tranquil lake. Large evergreen trees stood on the banks with their branches reaching out to dip into the water's edge. My mother motioned for me to sit on a nearby log encouraging me to simply observe, listen, and breathe deeply. While she did not refer to it as "forest bathing," and while I did not fully grasp its significance then, I was immersed in a world of wonder. All the elements and nuances of that forest at that moment converged to create a sense of peace and tranquility that has remained with me to this day.

Little did I know that this seemingly ordinary morning would become one of the most influential experiences of my life. It set in motion a lifelong passion for the natural world, leading me down the career path of a natural resource academic and a naturalist-interpreter. It also became my sanctuary, a mental haven where I sought solace and peace during life's turbulent moments. I find a profound resonance between my experience and the potent message that Maureen conveys in her book.

Fast forward to today when Maureen approached me with the request to compose this foreword for her book. A former remarkable student, later a respected colleague, and now a cherished friend of mine, she has penned a work of significance and practicality, one that not only delves into the depths of forest bathing but also masterfully weaves together the threads of heritage interpretation and the power of storytelling. She makes a seamless connection and delicate interplay between the practices of forest bathing and nature interpretation. As you read, you will discover that the membrane separating nature interpretation and forest bathing is as thin as the morning mist over a quiet lake.

Within the pages that follow, Maureen deftly interlaces historical accounts, scientific insights, and her own personal journey to paint a vivid portrait of why these practices are not merely relevant but imperative in our modern era. Through her words, we discover how this practice can transform our lives, offering a path to mental and emotional well-being in a world often filled with chaos, conflict, and noise. Her objective is crystal clear: to make this practice accessible, practical, and relatable to a diverse readership.

This book is more than just a guide to forest bathing; it is an invitation to rediscover our connection with nature, to immerse ourselves in its beauty, and to uncover the peace and inspiration that it offers. As you embark on this journey—as I did that fateful spring morning many years ago—may this book ignite a spark within you:

an aspiration to seek your own moments of forest bathing, to craft transformative experiences for others, and to uncover the serenity and rejuvenation that the natural world so generously bestows.

Maureen welcomes you to the world of forest bathing, where the boundaries between science and spirit, fact and folklore meld together, and the ancient wisdom of nature unfolds before you. Enjoy your journey into the forest.

Cem M. Basman, PhD

*"Two roads diverged in a wood and I—I took the road less traveled by and that has made all the difference."*

—Robert Frost

Chapter I

—

# INTRODUCING FOREST BATHING

When I first shared the idea of this book with a mentor, they read a few draft chapters and said they couldn't tell—was this a book about forest bathing or a book about interpretation? "Yes." I smiled, then explained, "It's a book about applying forest bathing as a tool to enhance interpretive style." After serving nearly three decades as a professional interpreter, I discovered the somatic practice of forest bathing and its undeniable lineage with the art of interpretation. Throughout my research to align sensory explorations with our interpretive standards, I took a deep dive into our interpretive archeology and noticed almost immediately that many, if not all, of our professional legends mention using the senses to reach our audiences. Forest bathing is an opening to sensory interpretation, and my intention through this book is to share ideas and spark interest in how to meld the two worlds to deliver outstanding opportunities for visitors and interpreters alike.

Forest bathing is a funny term that conjures weird imagery, cues jokes, and is a new concept to many of us. So, as we would a strange flower that suddenly caught our attention, let's begin by defining it. Notably, we are fast approaching the time when forest bathing won't need much of an introduction; because many of us will eventually be guided or learn about it from someone who has. If you haven't been guided yet, perhaps you have an imaginal sense of what the practice entails, or maybe you've only been aware of it recently and really don't know what it's all about. Regardless, with every gentle meander along a trail or heavy tromp through the woods, we've all been forest bathing this whole time, without ever calling it that.

Modern humans and the prehistoric species we evolved from have spent our existence in nature, yet the term forest bathing is just over four decades old in our contemporary vernacular. In just the past few years, there have been a myriad of articles and books published about forest bathing, and a growing worldwide legion of certified forest bathing guides—a profession and a practice referred to throughout this book as "guides" or "guiding." Amos Clifford, founder of the Association of Nature and Forest Therapy Guides and Programs (ANFT), is largely credited for bringing forest bathing to the United States upon launching the company in 2012. To date, over two thousand guides worldwide have been certified through ANFT by Clifford or one of his exceptional trainers.

For those of us impassioned with sharing its value, we look forward to days ahead when forest bathing becomes a part of our collective weekly health regimen. Once experienced, most folks don't need to be sold on forest bathing. Its benefits are easily recognizable.

So, what is forest bathing?

In 1982, Japan was undergoing a noticeable wave of mental and physical illnesses among its citizens. Likely causes were narrowed to environmental stressors, heightened urbanization, and a growing health epidemic somewhat reminiscent to what author Richard Louv would coin decades later as "nature-deficit disorder" in his book, *Last Child in the Woods: Saving our Children from Nature-Deficit Disorder* (2005. Chapel Hill, NC: Algonquin Books of Chapel Hill). The problems occurring in Japan mirrored what Louv later encapsulated through his work—the unhealthy work-school-life balance stemming from a mass retreat indoors to artificial light, bad indoor air quality, an overload of screen time, and severe deprivation of habitual aimless outdoor wandering. Japan's workforce was in overdrive.

It's strange to think of the '80s as being in the throes of a tech boom considering all our inventions and advances since, but certainly one was well underway. Back in the day when we welcomed the release of the Sony Walkman, I was in 5th grade and one of their 385 million happy consumers jamming down my block to the hits of the decade. In 1981, Japan became the largest manufacturer of Toshiba and Hitachi semiconductors, and Toshiba began marketing laptop computers that same year. Then in 1982, Japan rolled out the compact disc.

As all this is happening, Japan's Director of the Ministry of Agriculture, Forestry and Fisheries, Tomohide Akiyama, began pursuing the dual goals of renewing national interest in the nation's forestland while boosting ecotourism through enticing citizens to find mindfulness within the nation's sixty-five million acres of forestland. Guides began taking groups of people out on sensory explorations in the woods. In 1982, Akiyama coined the term *shinrin-yoku*, which translated means, "to bathe in the forest atmosphere." Forest bathing was born.

Apart from small distinctions, *shinrin-yoku*, forest therapy, forest bathing, nature therapy, woodland therapy, and silvo-therapy all essentially describe sensory immersion in nature. The words *shinrin-yoku* are written this way in the Kanji script:

森林浴

From the left, the first of the three characters that appear like three fat little trees clumped together symbolize forest, the middle character seems like two elongated trees signifying the interconnectedness of the forest, and the last of the three characters on the right resembles a roofed structure with water splashes referring to bath.

## The Journey of Forest Bathing

The practice of forest bathing varies from country to country, from landscape to landscape, and from guide to guide. Some guides take blood pressure readings for comparison before and after each program. Others offer pre and post Profile of Mood States (POMS) questionnaires to gauge change (POMS sample in Chapter 5). Forest bathing programs may have highly elaborate tea ceremonies, while others are very uncomplicated. Some are half-day or full weekend retreats; others might be shorter one-hour excursions (playfully referred to as "forest showers"). What remains consistent is that, like interpretive programs, forest bathing is accomplished in phases that fully establishes a beginning, middle, and end.

ANFT developed a standard sequence for guiding and a philosophy they call the "way of the guide," which reflects an attitude and approach to work that supports professional standards within the industry. The ANFT standard sequence provides a balanced combination of structure and predictability with room for a guide's creativity and adaptability to culture and circumstance.

The **tamed world** is where folks come from before they pull into the parking lot of the trailhead where the forest bathing program is set to begin. ANFT trainers Nadine Mazzola and Tam Willey interpreted the tamed world as an indispensable, yet restrictive part of the human condition. It consists of all the agreements, customs, and standards of living in a society with a reasonable degree of cooperation. The tamed world is where we live every day. It is essential; however, living in the tamed world often requires that we suppress parts of our wholeness—those parts that are not within the boundaries of what societies consider "normal."

**Hospitality** begins as soon as participants arrive on scene. It is a time to greet your guests, engage in casual conversations, and break the ice. Hospitality enables a guide to warmly welcome and assure them they have arrived at a safe place. An important element of Hospitality includes a short statement on holding reciprocity and kindness for the forest and for one another on a guided program. In 2009, I attended the very first meeting of Michigan's No Child Left Inside Coalition. Our event host was Tom Occhipinti of the Michigan Department of Environmental Quality (Ret.) who began our work by asking everyone to respect each other and honor different ideas. And Tom's lovely reminder struck me because I'd never heard anyone start a meeting like that: graciously laying the groundwork on how to support one another and welcome all stories. I always think of Tom when I share Hospitality in forest bathing, trying to mimic his natural ease and compassionate accompaniment for all of us while setting the stage.

The first phase is referred to as the **Threshold of Connection**, the way into the forest.

**Introduction** is a time to establish trust, explain the plan for the outing, how long you will be gone, a word about comforts such as restroom availability, and trail awareness such as poison ivy, slick surfaces, wildlife, etc. Let everyone know that invitations are optional. Guides then share land acknowledgments recognizing the original and current land tenders. Guides might also mention the watershed they are in. Finally, guides welcome the voices of the group for individual introductions.

**Pleasures of Presence,** also referred to as "embodied awareness," is a time to fully arrive in the forest; it is a time for participants to shake off the road dust of the tamed world, to slow down, and to invite people to get out of their heads and into their bodies. There is a fluidity to forest bathing—we bring our whole bodies into the land.

**What's In Motion?** This is a transitional invitation that involves a slow-moving stroll deeper into the forest. It's a good time to be "alone together" as participants notice what's in motion while moving silently down the trail. Participants are invited to share using the prompt "I am noticing" once the group reconvenes.

**Liminality.** The liminal journey of forest bathing involves moving from the "tamed world," which is where we are before arriving in the forest. Liminality is a place between space and time. It is not the tamed world, nor the wilderness, but the space in between.

**Invitations** are simple and sensory-orientated, and always offered as optional to participants. Sometimes guides pre-plan invitations, sometimes they use whatever is coming up, working in partnership with the land and the more-than-human world. Seasoned guides tap into what the land is offering at the time of the program. If it is windy, they share wind invitations. If there are many clouds, a cloud invitation is offered. Once returning to the group circle after each invitation, participants are again welcomed to share feedback using the prompt, "I am noticing."

**Tea ceremony** signals the conclusion of the program. It is a time to share reciprocity with the forest, gather and share with participants, and return from liminality to prepare to reenter the tamed world. All forest bathing outings begin and end with hospitality as a time for guides to hang out with participants, answer any burning questions folks are arriving or leaving with, and partake in casual convo on the way back to the parking lot.

ANFT describes the "way of the guide" as our individual attitudes toward the work. Guides don't control audiences, responses, or outcomes. A guide's role is to hold space like a vessel for people moving at their own pace. It's important to trust the process, trust the participants' capabilities, and trust the forest. Guiding is not about "me" or ego. Guides graciously open doors and welcome whatever arrives. It's important to remember that after a program, guides should feel relaxed and energized. Guiding should not be overly stressful or draining, and if it is, it's an indicator that the guide might be getting too involved in the outcome. This concept of letting go can be challenging for many park interpreters. I find myself in a perpetual state of overcompensating to help visitors feel welcomed and comfortable. With forest therapy I try and remove these behaviors from the equation because ultimately this practice is not about me or how the program is making *me* feel, it's about allowing participants the freedom to feel and do what they want to.

Chapter 5 provides a basic forest bathing example for new guides to practice and implement with groups. The chapter is meant as a basic framework for park interpreters to use, providing the standard sequence of forest bathing. After a while, new guides are encouraged to modify the example for their visitors. It is not necessary to use the exact invitations provided or have all the props and supplies mentioned. It is merely an example to be used as a springboard to tweak, alter, and revise in a way that makes sense to customize to style, location, and visitors.

## How Forest Bathing Is Good for Us

Phytoncides are natural antimicrobial allelochemical volatile organic compounds derived from plants. The Greek word phytoncide translates to "exterminated by the plant," or more literally, phyto=plant, cide=kill. It was coined in 1928 by Dr. Boris P. Tokin, a Russian biochemist from Leningrad University. Tokin discovered that some plants emit airborne chemicals that help to prevent them from rotting or being attacked by insects, bacteria, or fungus. These volatile chemical compounds are diffused by a variety of vegetative species—from deciduous and coniferous trees to small plants like garlic—and the molecular structures of phytoncides vary between species. Exposure to phytoncides have been associated with improvements in the activity of our frontline immune defenders.

Research also shows that forest bathing calms nervous system activity which prompts rest, conserves energy, and lowers blood pressure while increasing intestinal and glandular activity. In *The Hidden Life of Trees: What They Feel, How They Communicate* (2015. Vancouver, CA: Graystone Books), author Peter Wohlleben reminds us, "Every walk in the forest is like taking a shower in oxygen."

Ecologist and author, Dr. Paul A. Moore wrote about "The Endless River of Aroma" in his 2016 book, *The Hidden Power of Smell: How Chemicals Influence our Lives and Behavior* (2016. Bowling Green, OH: Springer). There Moore shared, "...exploring the smells of a fresh cut lawn, a spring rain, a fall forest, or even a warm pumpkin muffin is equally, and literally, breathtaking. Standing in the middle of an old growth forest as a gentle breeze delivers the aromas to my waiting nose, I am connected, deeply connected with the natural world."

Dr. Qing Li is an author, researcher, forest therapy guide, associate professor at the Nippon Medical School in Tokyo, and a world-renowned expert of nature and forest medicine. In his book, *Forest*

*Bathing: How Trees Can Help You Find Health and Happiness* (2018. New York, NY: Viking), Li shares details on his scientific experiments of incubating human Natural Killer (NK) cells with a phytoncide cocktail, and after a week or less, anti-cancer proteins had increased. This experiment was followed by Li's testing the effect of phytoncides on the immune responses of a dozen healthy, middle-aged men. Dr. Li found that exposure to phytoncides:

- significantly increased the numbers of NK cells and NK activity, as well as enhancing the activity of the anti-cancer proteins;
- significantly decreased the levels of stress hormones;
- increased the hours of sleep;
- decreased the scores for tension/anxiety, anger/hostility, and fatigue/confusion.

Dr. Li also points to a common harmless bacterium in soil called *Mycobacterium vaccae* that has been demonstrated in scientific research by the UK's Bristol University to stimulate the immune system and boost moods. The university provided sick mice with *M. vaccae* activating neurons in their immune systems, resulting in mice behaving as if they were on antidepressants. Even basic contact with the soil helps our bodies.

## Why Be Guided?

Once it's understood that anyone can forest bathe in any weather, in any place, in any way that feels right to them, one might ask, "Then what is the point of *being* guided?"

My annual *Forest Bathing for Women* at Oden State Fish Hatchery, Oden, Michigan.

One reason is that guides accompany and "hold time" to enable participants to fully engage in the practice. Often when we are outdoors alone and without an agenda, our mind begins to wander through the mildly nagging mental baggage from the tamed world: the dirty laundry left behind that needs attending, the banking yet to do, the grocery shopping, the overdue oil change, the unpaid bill, the doctor's appointment that needs to be made, the unanswered email, the meeting next week that we haven't prepared for, along with any deeper issues taking place in our lives. Under the weight of these thoughts, we might get antsy and want to leave, cut our outing short, or we may decide not to venture out at all—there are more important things to be doing! Guiding provides participants with the opportunity and the excuse to spend time outdoors which we might not otherwise afford ourselves.

Opening a forest bathing program with hospitality and introductions helps assure participants that their physical and emotional safety is important. Next, the participants need to know that the guide is trustworthy. Trustworthiness can also be established during hospitality and throughout the duration of the forest bathing program by honoring all stories, modeling ease, and witnessing. Choice is offered during each invitation and during sharing. Participants decide to engage in invitations any way that feels good to them or to not participate at all. This approach also enables participants' control of the experience through a collaborative effort with guides so that the forest bathing may be more effective. Finally, focusing on an individual's ability to lean into edges during programs empowers them to develop stronger coping skills.

When someone holds space and time for you, it helps lift you out of the mental gymnastics and keeps a focus on being back in your body and your senses. Being guided can help you learn a few techniques to replicate during a solo forest bathing outing.

Disconnecting from screen time and getting outside for health is something we've all been aware of for many years. Yet there are estimates that the average American adult now spends up to ten hours a day in front of a computer, TV, or their phone. Researchers from Harvard Medical School argue that beyond just raw hours spent, when and how people spend that time is more important to their brain's response. Research has discovered that screen time during different times of day or night affects sleep patterns, cognition, and memory, and dampens creativity and imagination. In 2010, research from the Keiser Family Foundation revealed that "Eight- to eighteen-year-olds spend more time with media than in any other activity besides (maybe) sleeping—an average of more than 7½ hours a day, seven days a week." The U.S. Centers for Disease Control and Prevention (CDC) created an online widget called Screen Time vs. Lean Time to provide ideas for parents to get kids outside and moving, and created an annual Screen Free Week schedule. Citizens can take the online pledge and register their event on an interactive national map. It's a step. Alas, even steps to become free of our screens for a short break invites our participation back to the screens.

In 2016, the French government wrote the El Khomri law (named after then French Minister of Labor, Madame Myriam El Khomri). Although controversial among labor groups, the law contains a progressive amendment referred to as the Adaptation of Work Rights to the Digital Era, Article 25, called *le droit à la déconnexion* or "the right to disconnect." Among other considerations, it affirms that employers with more than fifty employees are required by law to include information on this right in their Mandatory Annual Negotiation. Employers with less than fifty staffers are expected to document this right for them. Adoption of the right to disconnect has since spread to other countries within the European Union.

We are not quite there, yet in the U.S., we are inching towards protecting our time away from the office. I recently received an email from an employee with Michigan State University's Work/Life Office. At the bottom of the email, it read, "*If you are receiving this email outside of your typical working hours, I hope you feel no pressure to read or respond until your schedule and workload permit.*"

Another email response from a friend at Grand Rapids Pride read:

**Natureology**
@StineMaureen

···

**EUROPEAN OUT-OF-OFFICE:**

I'M AWAY CAMPING FOR THE SUMMER. PLEASE
EMAIL BACK IN SEPTEMBER.

**AMERICAN OUT-OF-OFFICE:**

I HAVE LEFT THE OFFICE FOR TWO HOURS TO
UNDERGO KIDNEY SURGERY BUT YOU CAN REACH
ME ON MY CELL ANY TIME.

8:35 AM · Mar 31, 2022 · Twitter Web App

"TRULY HUMAN NOTICE: Getting this email out of normal working hours? We work at a digitally enabled relentless pace, which can disrupt our ability to sleep enough, eat right, exercise, and spend time with people that matter the most. I am sending you this email at a time that works for me. I only expect you to respond to it when it is convenient to you."

One intent of forest bathing is escaping screen time to head outside and reconnect with our bodies and the land; it's imperative to our physical and mental well-being and so simple to engage in.

Taking two hours a week to lose track of time and be outside in nature yields a profound impact on your mental and physical health. And once you learn this method, you can share it with visitors while making the practice part of your weekly health regimen.

## Our Transformative Stories

Honoring all stories is a similar feature of both guiding and interpreting. Our stories evoke emotions and help us connect with our visitors and with each other. Sharing our stories together is an increasingly critical act during times when many of us feel we have no voice. Story sharing is healing. Story sharing can uplift us. Story sharing is a release. It helps in problem solving, breaking barriers, inspiring growth, and opens doors for story sharing by letting people know, *"Your voice matters."*

Ask any interpreter on earth, "Who is the father of heritage interpretation?" and they'll answer without pause, "Freeman Tilden." Our gang knows him well because the Massachusetts native made enormous contributions to advance the field of interpretation. An expert naturalist and accomplished author, Tilden is most famously known for his book, *Interpreting Our Heritage* (1957, 1967, 1977. Chapel Hill, NC: The University of North Carolina Press). In the pages of this brilliant work, Tilden shared the Six Principals of Interpretation that he developed which helped shape interpretive development and delivery for over a half-century. He is our north star.

The central premise of Larry Beck and Ted Cable's book, *Interpretation for the 21st Century: Fifteen Guiding Principles for Interpreting Nature and Culture, Second Edition* (2002. Champaign, IL: Sagamore Publishing) was to recap, slightly re-work, and add nine new principles to Freeman Tilden's original six. Chapter four of Beck and Cable's book elaborates on the fourth principal of interpretation and in it they write, "The purpose of the interpretive story, whether oral or written, is to prompt the listener or reader toward broadening his or her horizons and then acting on that newfound breadth." Beck and Cable go on to highlight "inspiration by example."

"The relationship of the interpreter to his or her subject, marked by a depth of knowledge and a sense of wonder, serenity, and fulfillment, is something that visitors will notice. They may inquire, on a personal level, how the interpreter can achieve these qualities in life, and they may, ultimately, try to emulate them."

Stories are personal experiences, beliefs, and philosophies that reach far beyond the individual. The principles of storytelling are equally paramount in interpretation and forest bathing. Guides and interpreters understand that participants bring their own stories and world perception to programming, and both professions recognize, create space, and welcome all stories. As professional story-sharers we create the containers—and allow space for many stories. We are not trying to get everyone to believe all stories but rather simply understand that different stories can co-exist.

In her work, *Braiding Sweetgrass: Indigenous Wisdom, Scientific Knowledge, and the Teachings of Plants* (2013. Minneapolis, MN: Milkweed Editions), author Robin Wall Kimmerer shared, "I am a listener and have been listening to stories told around me for longer than I care to admit. I mean to honor my teachers by passing on the stories that they have passed on to me. We are told that stories are living beings, they grow, they develop, they remember, they change not in their essence, but sometimes in their dress. They are shared and shaped by the land and the culture and the teller, so that one story may be told widely and differently. Sometimes only a fragment is shared, showing just one face of a many faceted story, depending on its purpose…*Chi Megwech* to the storytellers."

This book is a collection of stories including my interpretive travelogue of recovery and discovery applying forest bathing to the art of interpretation. My goal is to provoke programming creativity for those of us who lead public programs by applying the healing practice of forest bathing and cultivating sensory interpretation as a foundation to improve interpretive style and hone new interpretive audiences. Interpreters can approach my invitation to grow in our craft through weaving a few sensory activities into an existing program, which I refer to as sensory interpretation from ideas shared in Chapter 4, and/or to offer forest bathing as a stand-alone addendum to their current programming repertoire by using the example outlined in Chapter 5.

I dedicate these stories to fellow early adopters of all backgrounds, all disciplines, all stages of a career or post-career. To you my cousins, who run straight through the fire to the triumphs. My overarching purpose is to inspire anyone to engage in forest bathing for personal renewal—to become their own shape shifters, lighten their load, and indulge in forest bathing for restoration, relaxation, and grounding. We've been through a lot in recent years and it's time for a breather. Thank you for joining me for some outdoor wandering together. The trees await us.

### Case Study: Forest Wayfinding with Persons Who Are Blind or Low Vision

At our summer camp for children and young adults who are blind or have low vision, we utilize forest bathing techniques for wayfinding. Because our campers (and most of our staff) cannot use their eyes to find trails or identify where they are, they must use their other senses—hearing, touch, smell, and yes, even taste—to find their way. This can result in an almost inadvertent enjoyment and spiritual connection with the woods.

Many people who are blind or low vision are afraid of the natural environment. Insects are particularly problematic because a blind person cannot identify the kind of insect that is landing on them or buzzing around them; even butterflies can be terrifying for some because of their large size and unpredictable flight patterns. Obviously, mosquitos, wasps, bees, and biting flies pose danger. Fear of contacting poison ivy is also deeply imbedded in some of our campers' and staff minds, so it is critical that the person leading a session in the woods has the knowledge to avoid as many of these challenges as possible.

When we go into the forest, we prepare with insect repellant, sturdy shoes, and hopefully long sleeves, socks, and long pants. This allows our campers and staff to concentrate on the woods around them instead of worrying about potential damage to their skin caused by insects, ticks, branches, brambles, and such.

Our kids and staff use their white canes to identify the trail. If they tap middle to side, they will find packed earth in the center and leaves or taller grasses to the side. They will find the path is either packed earth or short grass under their feet. They are encouraged to feel the earth under their feet and their connection to the natural world.

As we meander along, we talk about the kinds of plants growing in certain areas of the forest—what grows where a large tree has recently fallen, what is now eating that downed tree, what grows on the edges of a clearing, what grows in dense shade. We identify those plants by leaf shape and size, size of the plant, presence of thorns, and any interesting fruit or seed pods it might be growing, like May Apples. We identify clearings by paying attention to air currents on our faces—a clearing feels very different from dense woods. We think about the heaviness of the air in a heavily wooded environment. We talk about why the air feels and smells different in different places. We listen for different kinds of birds and insects in different areas of our trail— whether the clearing or the deep forest or somewhere in between. We talk about why it would be difficult for a large bird, like a barred owl or a red-tailed hawk, to fly in the deep woods. We listen for the variety of ways different kinds of trees rustle in the breeze—pines do not sound at all like a grove of oaks! When we come to a stream, we encourage the kids to lie flat on the bridge and feel the water, describe it, and think about where it has come from and where it is going, and what it is doing for its part on the earth. We talk about what creatures we might find near the creek and why—frogs, toads, salamanders, and snakes, plus a huge assortment of insects.

Sometimes we find things we can taste. Raspberries and blackberries are our favorites! Sometimes we are lucky enough to find wintergreen, wild strawberries, Queen Anne's Lace, and other plants to taste and/or smell. We also talk about invasive species, like garlic mustard and autumn olive.

The more they know about the natural world around them, the less fearful they are. Once we have learned about the sources of the sounds and textures and smells of the woods, they can relax a bit.

We often just stand, listen, feel, and pay attention to our bodies and minds and the world around us that we often ignore or skip because we are too busy. This is hard for some of our kids; they don't like just being still! It's uncomfortable for them. But the more we do it, the more they like it, and the more they are able to master the urge to move constantly as they take time to listen to the earth, to feel the earth, to smell the earth, and taste the earth. When you are a blind person, you have a different relationship to the world than a sighted person, but it is one worth thinking about as valuable for all of us to ignore what we see and pay attention to our other senses.

Gwen Botting | Executive Director of Opportunities Unlimited for the Blind, Michigan. *Photos by Sheila Wing-Proctor (left and right) and Mo Stine (center).*

*"It is easier to build strong children than to repair broken men."*
—Frederick Douglass, 1855

# Chapter 2

---

## PANARCHY HAPPENS

So much goes into the lifelong work of becoming a "good" interpreter. Some basic tenets that certainly apply to any industry include time, energy, humility, dedication, opportunity, research, trial and error, and perhaps most importantly, encountering fabulous mentors along the trail to demonstrate the way of our craft and all its nuance. Ralph Waldo Emerson said, "Our chief want is someone who will inspire us to be what we know we could be." I began my interpretive career path in 1995, and throughout the decades, I've been lucky to have several amazing influencers.

My first boss, the late George Poulos of the Chicago Park District, embodied a natural virtuosity interpreting parks and recreation within the third largest urban complex in the nation. Mr. Poulos's infectious love for music, kids, and community was my poignant catalyst. In the Shawnee National Forest of Southern Illinois my boss, Patricia York, showed me how to deliver interpretive public tours of the historic

Celebrating another incredible day in the high desert with my colleague, Rhonda, at Craters of the Moon National Monument, Arco, Idaho, during its 75th anniversary, 1999.

My amazing assistant, Marisa Warchol (left) and I enjoying our workday at Wolf Lake State Fish Hatchery, Mattawan, Michigan, 2001. *Photo by Martha Wolgamood.*

Ox-lot Cave as we descended its sandstone steps along the Rim Rock National Recreation Trail. Deep beneath the Snake River Plain of Southeastern Idaho my boss, Doug Owen, taught me how to interpret volcanology for park visitors while crawling on our bellies throughout the cool, dark caverns of ancient lava flows at Craters of the Moon National Monument. From the bow I studied how to interpret the brackish ecology of the Pamlico Sound for our young campers from my boss, Desta Hudson, as we paddled past resident cottonmouths up the Neuse River in Eastern North Carolina. During my tenure as director of the Wolf Lake State Fish Hatchery Visitor Center, the value of keeping multiple irons in the fire to forge meaningful partnerships and reflect excellence in visitor services was expertly demonstrated by my boss, Sarah Reding, in Southwest Michigan. And through the gracious leadership of my boss, Dr. Francie Cuthbert, I was artfully schooled on the life history of the endangered Great Lakes piping plovers in hopes of provoking trespassing anglers toward a conservation mindset for these plump little shoreline specialists at the paradise that is Wilderness State Park in Northern Lower Michigan.

For many years during this winding journey, I continuously hit the jackpot with incredibly inspiring interpretive supervisors. They applauded my successes but never let me off the hook, telling me when I messed up, fully expecting hard work and exponential growth in return, each giving me a master class in human grace. George, Patricia, Doug, Desta, Sarah, and Francie possessed innate leadership talents nurturing my career, providing sage advice, supporting my day-to-day

Clowning around with my colleagues (l-r): Sofa-Marcus, (*Alice's puppy*), Charlotte, Jen, Andrea, Ian, me sprawled over them. Floor-Alice and Electra at the Don Lee Environmental Education Center, Arapahoe, North Carolina. 2000. *Photo by Desta Hudson.*

progress, and sharing their gifts amidst the most breathtaking American landscapes whose beauty is forever imprinted within me.

Throughout my travels I also enjoyed celebratory times with talented, aspiring interpretive coworkers. We loved the art of interpretation, the visitors, and sharing the story of where we worked. We loved creating, planning, developing, and implementing interpretive public programs and academic curriculum and we were hyper-focused on it. We loved pursuing professional certifications and attending workshops and conferences to grow our network. Many of us became lasting friends, uplifting each other, practicing our craft together, and I was proud of our contributions.

As a young park interpreter, I discovered that I had a talent for interpreting fishing to kids and building their confidence through fishing. It is my superpower. From practice on the hard water and off summer fishing piers, I came to understand the proper way to safely handle large, heavy fish, anticipating the timing and strength of a trout's

Fishing with friends from the Little Traverse Bay Bands of Odawa Indians on Crooked Lake, Emmet County, Michigan. *Photo by Alison Adams.*

strong muscles when they thrashed violently back and forth to get free, and I helped new anglers understand this skill. I demonstrated to little fingers exactly how firmly to grip the fish around the solid, thick space before the tail without harm by holding on with the dominant hand, and the precise way to safely palm the other hand between the belly and the lower jaw supporting the body horizontally without touching the bright red gills to avoid the fish bleeding out. I covered some essentials like how to carefully remove the hook with hemostats. How to gently return a fish to the water holding onto the tail and guiding it back and forth slowly to revive it before letting go. How to leave no trace near a body of water by picking up empty bait containers, discarded monofilament, and lunch wrappers—no matter who left them. I've witnessed the proud look wash over faces when kids finally landed a fish, an incredible feat of their young lives, immediately followed by high-fives and happy pictures showing off their catch next to their parents, aunts, uncles, grandmas, and grandpas. There is nothing like it.

Landing a lunker with a trout buddy at Pond Hill Farm, Harbor Springs, Michigan. *Photo by Andrea Stine.*

The experiences gave me profound and deep satisfaction knowing I was exactly where I needed to be doing exactly what I was meant to do. But there came a time when my interpretive career survived an unimaginable cataclysmic implosion. I watched helplessly as my life's work—and my joy—circled the drainpipe. The episode was indelibly gutting, its devastation visceral, and for a long time afterwards, I fully disconnected from things I used to welcome. Looking down from where I landed, I know that the trauma I weathered then ultimately revealed my path to forest bathing. The practice is an available tool providing a gentle convalescence where healing takes place between the forest as the therapist, and the participant. Mindfulness in nature through forest bathing not only inspired my work fostering sensory interpretation, it irrefutably enhanced my interpretive style, taught me how to slow my roll, focus on the long game, and most importantly, helped me reclaim my sense of self.

## Be Best

In my thirty-third year I sent down a tap root. I stopped traveling and bought my first house after being hired as a full-time, year-round park interpreter. And outcompeting dozens of other candidates for the job made it my small mid-career miracle. The process started with the customary writing of a cover letter, updating my resume, submitting the application packet, followed by two song-and-dance interviews in front of a conspicuously large panel of onlookers judging my every move within the smallest and warmest room possible. Commendations rolled in from nationwide references, a criminal background search was conducted, my fingerprints were analyzed in the federal database, and then a final critical hurdle: the meticulous scrutiny of my pee's temperature and chemistry. Because no way were they about to hire a park interpreter hopped up on abstract creativity and Cherry Garcia.

Upon deeming my waste matter sufficiently boring, I finally got the call, and I was over the moon. Happy, insured, and permanent, I began my new post excited to dive right in. And that's exactly what I did, absorbing each detail about the site and fully immersing myself in learning all I could with grace and gratitude. But it didn't take long to figure out that like many in this field, I was expected to do far more than simply interpret. Charged with pioneering the historic facility's first interpretive services program, launching its inaugural visitor center, and organizing a community Friends Group, my time was spent juggling excellence in interpretation with replacing disintegrating urinal cakes and selling foregone landfill from the center's gift store. I rushed around the place with one hand on a prop and the other on a mop and timeouts were often hard to come by.

Now and then I took to wander our trails for some reprieve, but breaks were usually cut short by those critical fires to put out like confirming the cost of a rubber tomahawk missing its price tag or helping my team find the lost key to the bathroom supplies closet. I exhausted my days trying to inspire grossly underpaid support staff and safely host hundreds of national and international tourists, per-forming hourly triage for visitors' bee stings, heat stroke, and hiking injuries because meeting the rigor of the job is what I signed up for and I owned it. It was sink or swim, and with very little guidance, I learned quickly how to tackle unpredictable challenges, striking that delicate balance between toilets and Tilden delivering outstanding visitor experiences.

Still, I began to realize that an ominous undercurrent of my employment meant surviving an astonishingly hostile workplace fomented by bored, jealous, emotional leadership coaching their minions to punch down. I stepped into this new space expecting an uplifting professional atmosphere managed with an equality lens until three weeks into my job, one minion shared their unsolicited gospel that I was leading an "alternative lifestyle" by existing in my thirties unmarried without children. Sometime later, another insisted we go around the breakroom table one at a time and openly declare our stance on same-sex marriage. Eventually it came my turn to answer. The lone egalitarian in the room, I fell under immediate suspicion over my inability to harbor judgmental prejudice against marginalized communities. And afterwhile labeled and shunned for my failure to laugh at cruelty, my lack of racial intolerance, my crime of being hired for a position in a state I didn't hail from, my personal life, my salary range, and my sustained disinterest in procreating the species—all of which outrageous and none of which in any remote way mattered to the interpretive work I was delivering to help others shine.

Bullied by the very people I was hired to publicly celebrate, when I took issue, its severity gradually intensified. We had the best jobs that were the envy of many. Their choice could have been to focus purely on themselves. Ignore me, avoid me, enjoy everyday life. But my colleagues—grown adults raising young children—made easy work of their brutality, writing partisan slogans antithetical to my views with their fingertips through road dirt on my car windows, leaving ugly notes with nicknames for me in clearly identifiable handwriting on my office desk, vandalizing my interpretive signs with profanities, and smearing my interpretive props with animal blood. Most deplorable was their ringleader: a classic careerist demagogue, regularly referring to me as the "Jew-girl" and informing me, *"That's just the Jew in you"* anytime I asked questions that involved my concern about anything.

Filled with dread and a victim's common reluctance to come forward, I found the courage to tell my lead worker. Rather than a warranted litany of formal apologies, pink slips, and supportive professional mediation, the official response was to hold a cosplay kangaroo court to interrogate me over someone else's bigotry without any human resources officers in attendance. Actually back-slapping themselves when they finished for a job well done. Malignant narcissists are skilled at pathologizing reactions to abuse, persuading others that the reaction is the actual problem over the abuse itself. Demonstrably biased, inner circle headquarter galaxy brains were preternaturally convinced that their disgusting racism was some freakish joke between the two of us, because of course I enjoyed being a target of xenophobia equal to the individual spewing it—as one does. Pure traumady.

Least but not last, because opportunities were scarce during my daily tour of duty, I robbed myself of my scheduled time off to relax and recharge, instead planning events and programs for work. I slept with a pen and pad on my bedside table for the wheels that never stopped turning, dreaming up new interpretive methods to try out on our visitors, arriving at work hours before my shifts began to clean the massive outdoor exhibits and get a jump start on each day. And I behaved like this because interp is my jam. I foolishly thought that if I just kept up this pace—keeping the tops of the bathroom stalls free of dust and burning the hours of my personal time—my work product would without a doubt help me rise above the systemic herd mentality; eventually they'd recognize the value I brought to the table and then it wouldn't matter how I voted, who I loved, what I believed in.

All I wanted was to teach little kids how to fish, so becoming a paid janitor and volunteer docent—under the guise of "park interpreter"— within the most unaccountable, toxic worksite imaginable was somehow worth the price of admission. Ignoring the flashing red signals to recalibrate, I began a slow descent, collapsing under the weight of speed and time sickness. American doctors consider this pattern a backslide toward hypertension, heart disease, or stroke. The Japanese call it *karoshi* 過労死 or death by overwork.

It took a long time to unravel how I got here. Up until this chapter, I repeatedly landed and thrived in sound, safe, stable worksites with accomplished bosses that stood by me. Although there were plenty of busy, stressful days along my path, for this I held no point of reference, no previous training, and because the repugnant work culture was so fully metastasized up the food chain, no mentor to help me figure out how to cope. Instead, it was explained to me that I was up against The Chosen Ones—insular staff who displayed keenly unique personality traits useful to their virulent middle manager thereby shielding them from fallout of their incendiary workplace behavior through a de facto permission structure. "Short of physical assault," my lead worker further warned me, "you'll never win any fight [*sic*] here."

Thus, my protesting their malevolence was considered "fighting." Worse, these individuals I worked alongside every day had to inflict bodily harm upon me before administration would be forced to act. Assault and battery was the clear line in the sand. Everything beneath this *Lord of the Flies* threshold was encouraged, rewarded, and as such, persisted. Crestfallen and with a heaviness I carried inside me nonstop, it was surreal knowing I had invested a decade of my life earning the professional credentials to qualify to *even apply* for this dream job, let alone land it and once hired, gradually breaking myself to prove I belonged. I was trapped in a deflating professional death spiral, and I became a pariah.

Distant colleagues working outside the confines of this bedlam, aware of the insidious abuse I was facing, were repelled by it. A few shared their private empathies with me. Some I considered friends disappeared into the ether. I couldn't blame them. It's possible many feared that if they called bullshit over what was happening to me, they'd get into their own good trouble. And so, my demise was witnessed in soft whispers and deafening silence. With neither natural beauty nor political connections to sway the betas, I relied on energy and ambition to carry me. But nothing made a difference. Not authoring innovative statewide school curricula, not implementing successful interpretive programs, not building strong, enduring community partnerships, not mentoring younger staffers, not accruing hundreds of hours of unclaimed overtime, not seventy-eight months of springing for breakroom donuts, not the diurnal frozen smile plastered on my face, not sparkling bathroom floors, not in fact *being* a gentile.

My seminal moment came the day a local union leader arrived at my worksite following my request for representation. I was called to an ambiguous personnel meeting by upper echelon that morning and this time I invited my union for protection. We said hello, and my rep proceeded to tell me that they were not allowed to attend the meeting. "My hands are tied," they explained, "until or unless you break a work rule, I cannot physically be in the room to represent you for this." Then they hugged me, we said goodbye, and as I watched them turn and leave it happened.

What arrived was a liberating flood of interpersonal awareness as it finally dawned on me that altruism, expertise, and crullers weren't going to help me withstand this environment. We were done here. I was "the other" whose very presence defied ingrained myopic worldviews and upset delicate sensibilities, and regardless of what I accomplished or how hard I worked to avoid this outcome, I would never be accepted. Despite everything, I held genuine hope for the daughters of my coworkers, who once grown, would feel kindness and fellowship at work and elsewhere. All of their daughters. No matter what.

For my part, I'd been prolonging the workplace turmoil by failing to set my own boundaries, to find my voice, to work my grit, to defend my personhood, to hire legal counsel.

I stopped living deliberately. I lost me.

### Per Aspera Ad Astra

Not long after leaving this job, a small group of professionals who comprised my state's Project Learning Tree (PLT) committee

Accepting the National PLT Outstanding Educator Award, Pt. Clear, Alabama, 2013. *Photo by Ada Takacs.*

nominated me as the PLT State Educator of the Year, and this honor was followed by the accolade of National Outstanding Educator of Project Learning Tree. When I got the news, I was floored—they typically reserve that recognition exclusively for formal teachers. My gut reaction called to mind a line from Daniel Defoe's *Robinson Crusoe*, **"For sudden joys, like griefs,** confound at first."

The national award came with a complimentary trip to Oregon to study at the International Educator's Institute of the World Forestry Center (WFC). Rick Zenn, senior fellow at WFC, was our guide and instructor for this innovative peer-to-peer professional development program. Through the coursework we were provided hands-on field visits focused on outcome-driven collaboration of best practices in conservation education, and the interrelated social, economic, and environmental challenges facing the earth's forests. This intensive forest study tour was comprised of experienced multicultural leaders actively working in education, research, natural resource management

The International Educator's Institute, of the World Forestry Center, class of 2013 in the foreground of the majestic Mt. Hood. Oregon. *Photo by Rick Zenn.*

and strategic communication. There were twenty-one of us in the class and collectively we hailed from China, Iran, Taiwan, India, Bosnia and Herzegovina, Armenia, Nigeria, Estonia, Uganda, Finland, Cameroon, and several states across the U.S.

During our time together, Zenn introduced us to panarchy, a centuries-old complex theory named after the mythical Greek god of nature, Pan, who is half-man half-goat and whose very persona serves as an icon of unpredictable change.

To demonstrate the theory, Zenn took us to Mount St. Helens National Volcanic Monument and our class watched a film on the historic 1980 eruption and the incredible transformation and rebirth of flora and fauna that rapidly took shape across the devastated landscape.

Zenn furthered our lesson by introducing us to the book, *The Upside of Down: Catastrophe, Creativity, and the Renewal of Civilization* (Homer-Dixon. 2006. Toronto, CA: Vintage Canada). In this work,

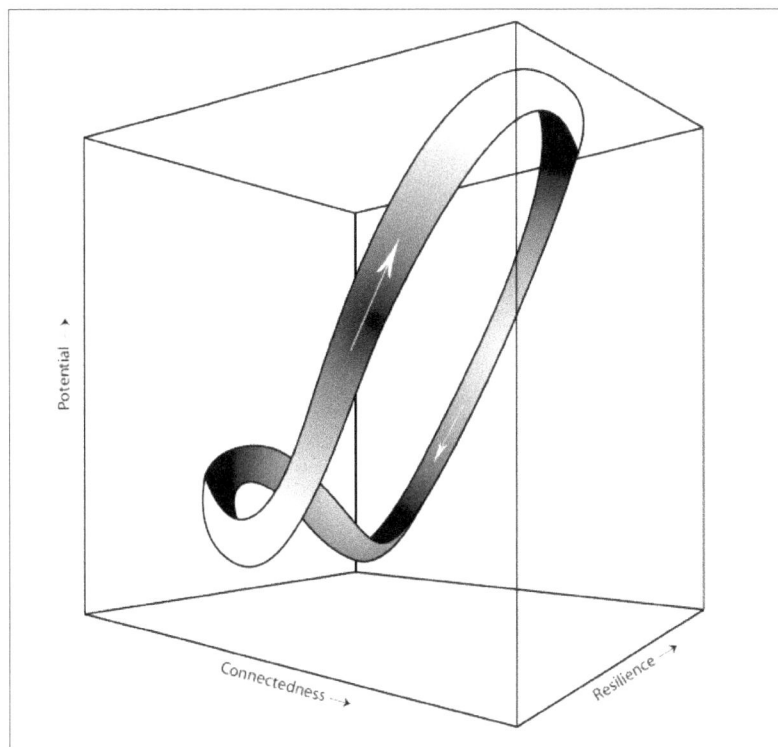

The 3-D Adaptive Cycle, T. Homer-Dixon. Reprinted with permission.

author, professor, and researcher Dr. Thomas Homer-Dixon examines the adaptive cycle, "…in these ways the forest ecosystem reorganizes and regenerates itself, quite possibly in a very new form. Put simply, the catastrophe of collapse allows for the birth of something new. And this cycle of growth, collapse, reorganization, and rebirth allows the forest to adapt over the long term to a constantly changing environment."

The theory is far broader, but I simplify panarchy to explain how people, like forests, are able to go through disaster and yet bounce back. Once the dust settles, something quite remarkable happens and life not only begins again, but often stronger with more resilience than before the crisis. Panarchy illustrates the simultaneous traits of consistency and transformational change in complex systems.

Civilizations, forests, careers, and even our personal lives are thankfully all susceptible to transformation. Amidst collapse, it's hard to imagine things will change, let alone improve. The adaptive cycle is a recurring dance between turmoil and order, and our internal systems—the whole of who we are—has not only the capacity to roll with the changes but fully respond to these opportunities through growth and innovation. We don't typically appreciate life's detours when we initially encounter them, but often they hit us like cathartic release—a gigantic exhale after holding our breath for too long. Out of darkness and onto amazing summits.

Maybe you are experiencing a similar reorganization.

In her book, *The Politics of Trauma* (2019. Berkeley, CA: North Atlantic Books), author Staci K. Haines devotes Chapter 4 to discussing the impact of trauma and oppression, "Traumatic experiences and oppressive social conditions cause us to move into a series of automatic, holistic, and incredibly creative means of first surviving then adapting to the harm, ruptured connection with ourselves and others and betrayal. We are built for safety, belonging, and dignity. We are built to be connected to, and make a difference for others, to have meaningful lives. When any of these core needs are disrupted through trauma, we automatically attempt to protect ourselves. We instinctively adapt. To the superficial gaze, it may not look like adaption, but with a deeper view, it becomes understandable and obvious."

Professional forest bathing guides are trained to uphold the five guiding principles of trauma-informed care (TIC). Those principles are safety, trustworthiness, choice, collaboration, and empowerment. We use a heart-centered approach throughout the practice, which includes, among other things, listening, trusting, open-mindedness, compassion, and believing in the goodness of humanity.

In the years following my workplace harassment—which at the time my UAW Local 6000 referred to as "violence in the workplace"—a growing number of employers now validate the importance of the overall health of their employees through employee check-ins, wellness action plans, and sharing meaningful resources. The era of fragile office thugs, their shrugs, and *It is what it is* is slowly dying.

One notable example of progress in workplace safety resulted from the first civil rights law of the 21st century called the No FEAR Act. Passed by the 107th Congress of the United States and signed into law on May 15, 2002, as Public Law, 107-174, the No FEAR Act stands for, Notification and Federal Employee Antidiscrimination and Retaliation Act of 2002, and although imperfect, the law protects federal employees from federal managers and supervisors from engaging in unlawful discrimination and retaliation.

Two decades later on October 20, 2022, Dr. Vivek Murthy, the 21st Surgeon General of the United States, addressed our nation's workplace mental health crisis for the very first time in our history. The US Department of Health and Human Services released the *Surgeon General's Framework for Workplace Mental Health and Well-Being*, a thirty-page guide created to help organizations develop, institutionalize, and update policies, processes, and practices that best support the mental health and well-being of all workers. "We have an opportunity and the power to make workplaces engines for mental health and well-being," Surgeon General Vivek Murthy said in a statement. "It will require organizations to rethink how they protect workers from harm, foster a sense of connection among workers, show workers that they matter, make space for their lives outside work, and support their growth. It will be worth it because the benefits will accrue for workers and organizations alike." The Framework highlights five essentials for workplaces.

From their website:

1. Protection from Harm: Creating the conditions for physical and psychological safety is a critical foundation for ensuring mental health and well-being in the workplace. In order to promote practices that better assure protection from harm, workplaces can:
    a. Prioritize workplace physical and psychological safety
    b. Enable adequate rest
    c. Normalize and support focusing on mental health

    d. Operationalize Diversity, Equity, Inclusion, and Accessibility (DEIA) norms, policies, and programs

2. Connection and Community: Fostering positive social interaction and relationships in the workplace supports worker well-being. In order to promote practices that better assure connection and community, workplaces can:
    a. Create cultures of inclusion and belonging
    b. Cultivate trusted relationships
    c. Foster collaboration and teamwork

3. Work-Life Harmony: Professional and personal roles can create work and non-work conflicts. In order to promote practices that better assure work-life harmony, workplaces can:
    a. Provide more autonomy over how work is done
    b. Make schedules as flexible and predictable as possible
    c. Increase access to paid leave
    d. Respect boundaries between work and non-work time

4. Mattering at Work: People want to know that they matter to those around them and that their work matters. Knowing you matter has been shown to lower stress, while feeling like you do not can increase the risk for depression. In order to better assure a culture of mattering at work, workplaces can:
    a. Provide a living wage
    b. Engage workers in workplace decisions
    c. Build a culture of gratitude and recognition
    d. Connect individual work with organizational mission

5. Opportunities for Growth: When organizations create more opportunities for workers to accomplish goals based on their skills and growth, workers become more optimistic about their abilities and more enthusiastic about contributing to the organization. In order to promote practices that better assure opportunities for growth, workplaces can:
    a. Offer quality training, education, and mentoring
    b. Foster clear, equitable pathways for career advancement
    c. Ensure relevant, reciprocal feedback

"Our workplaces play a significant role in our lives and can impact our physical and mental well-being—in good ways and bad…The Surgeon General's Framework is a guide to call attention to a public health issue, developed to help the American public better understand and address factors that affect health. This Framework provides Essentials, a foundation of key components, for workplace leaders to engage all workers and equitably support their mental health and well-being. It includes evidence-informed practices that leadership across workplaces of varied sizes and industries can apply to reimagine and reinvigorate their organizations."

## Interpreting Somatics

Understanding somatics plays an important role in wellness and recovery from trauma. The term soma is a Greek root word which means "the whole self" and practitioners of somatics contend that the body, the whole self and all our moods, mindsets, feelings, action, and inaction fall under the same category. The body is our whole self. Once we tune in to our body, we can make holistic, transformational changes felt across many areas of our lives.

Adopting somatics begins with considering our shape. Shape in this context is not physical but who we are, how we present ourselves, what embodies us. Shape contains emotions, lived moments, habits, values, and all the things we do and chose not to do.

Somatics is a methodology for change. We can alter our current trajectory if we care to by amending our shape through somatics using a three-part phase I learned from Staci K. Haines.

Somatic *awareness* prompts us to ask, what are you noticing in sensations and in your body? When we drop our attention into our whole system, we can gain more information about ourselves. Not only listening to our brain but using all of our senses to pay attention to our body.

Somatic *opening* is transforming from one shape to a different shape that's more aligned with what we care about and what we want to become. Notice and open shifting pathways and emotions to what we want to be, allowing more choice.

Somatic *practice* means that we become what we practice; we are always practicing something. Consider if what you are currently practicing aligns with what you want to bring to the world, what you most care about, what you want to accomplish, what you hope to reflect. Somatic practices like forest bathing help us move towards what we most care about and what we want to be. These practices help us redirect our triggered reactions, and when stressful encounters happen, we can lean into somatic practices to better guide our responses and outcomes. It helps us build the tools and skills to think deeper about our body, beyond merely a vehicle to get you from here to there. Practice creates sustainability.

How we apply the somatic practice of forest bathing is by slowing down in nature, being still, and start noticing what we are drawn to. There's that word again: noticing. Noticing takes focus and blocks out distractions. Noticing does not mean analyzing, obsessing, or overthinking. Noticing also does not imply that we ignore grief by burying it deep inside ourselves. It means sitting with all manner of thoughts and feelings, good and bad. Simply noticing.

Practicing somatics enhanced my interpretive career and helped restore my serenity and feelings of self-worth in several ways.

First, I started to alter my anguished shape through establishing clean measurable goals. This began with a return to surrounding myself with humans that aimed to impact positive change and who concerned themselves with little else. During the dark years, I shrugged off insolence like water off a wood duck's back. My poor, early reactions to the caustic-adjacent was go along to get along. But over time, aloof, bombastic leadership who fell ass backwards into their positions grew easy to recognize by their manner of speech and deeds; flashy, transparent, spineless-admirers bent on impressing other inauthentic agency bros through abject misogyny and slander. Rather than relying on tolerance and acceptance as my defense mechanisms for baser-minded management wallowing in their disfunction, I practiced putting myself and my interests first. I stopped seeing my job as the whole of my identity. I changed my shape through revitalizing my roots using muscle memory of working on fruitful projects with inspiring, thoughtful people who genuinely cared about our collective successes.

Next, I wanted to change what I expected from an employer. Beyond being gratified for having a job, I rewired my thinking. They were lucky to have me. My gifts. My energy. My experience. My outlook. My attitude. I began to mandate mutualism from employers. This involved careful listening, gauging the temperature, questioning, and taking stock in answers during interviews and early days on a new job. I wanted to know the mood going in and I stayed vigilant in my existential right to create in peace. In short, I got really picky about where I worked, deciding to always put my health and happiness first—a pact with myself that I continue to keep alive today.

Organizational psychologist, professor, and *New York Times* best-selling author, Robert Sutton wrote about why every workplace should be asshole-free in his 2007 classic, *The No Asshole Rule*. Bob recently shared his thoughts with me about workplace assholes: "We now have thousands of studies that show assholes undermine the mental and physical health of the people around them, stifle effort and innovation, and cause the best people to quit. Sure, some assholes finish first, but it is usually despite rather than because of their cruelty. In my book, if you are a winner and an asshole, you are still a loser as a human being because you leave so much destruction in your wake."

In her 2013 masterpiece, *How Not to Be a Dick*, author and artist, Meghan Doherty reminds us, "Throughout history, there have been dicks…Dicks don't stop to consider how their attitudes, actions and words affect other people. Dicks are, as a rule selfish and thoughtless. They take out their fears, frustrations, insecurities, and ignorance on others…and recognizing dickishness in action is the first step toward minimizing the overall impact of dickishness in the world."

My path to wellness at work galvanized through adopting sensory interpretation which manifested when discovering somatics which emerged by practicing forest bathing which ignited upon learning about panarchy which grew from the ashes of a traumatic professional nightmare instigated by a small dickish gang of belligerent assholes.

## Wander Where Wi-Fi Is Weak

Consider what you are currently practicing. How might sensory interpretation and forest bathing change your somatic shape?

Maybe you want to be a better park interpreter. Begin by noticing what it looks like to be "better." Does it mean growing a deeper knowledge about your subject matter? Spending more time on your research? Working with decent coworkers? Being able to better connect with your audience? Does it mean developing a more entertaining interpretive delivery? Applying for jobs that yield advancement? Trying something new and edgy like interpretive writing? Is it sharing respect with supervisors? Perhaps you simply want to improve how you show up for your visitors during a stressful workday.

The somatic practice of exploring the senses through forest bathing for oneself or to share is undisputedly healthy for the system. Likewise, it's a solid first step to engage in forest bathing alone before field testing it on an audience. Agenda-free time outdoors is part of the recovery process. Repairing a relationship to place is important even if you are not suffering from damaging moments from your past or the present. Wandering in the woods is good medicine free to the seeker and ever available. Some might question why interpreters who seemingly spend the bulk of our time out-of-doors would need forest bathing to recharge and restore. But even those of us in a supportive network with quality leaders benefit from a nature boost for ourselves. Even those of us serving as professional interpreters without the added responsibility of a visitor center or staff to manage are inundated with demands of vast amounts of screen time: answering/sending emails, scanning/uploading documents, participating in Zoom/Teams/Skype meetings, graphic designing, endless social media posting, and every corner of our profession occupying our headspace or pulling us indoors. Yet often when outdoors, we are busy with groups, implementing interpretive programs on fishing, forests, wildlife, history, focused on our talk, our goals and expectations, answering rapid-fire questions, making sure the group is safe and the resource is protected from group behavior. Despite being outdoors, we can be stuck in our minds and forget to remember to pause and evoke the senses.

Ferris State University professor Cindy Fitzwilliams-Heck reminds us in her work, *A Practical Guide to Nature Study, Third Edition* (2021. Dubuque, IA: Kendall Hunt Publishing Co) that nature may help us feel "unstuck." "When you find yourself mentally blocked," shares Fitzwilliams-Heck, "try time outdoors walking around with no agenda except to be present in the moment…the sights, sounds, smells, and textures can translate into many forms of artistic interpretations. Experiences outdoors can inspire you in ways that may be unexpected."

By letting go and getting out of the tamed world for a few hours every week we can often encounter, remember, and incorporate those outcast parts of ourselves when we connect deeply with nature.

If you are not already reading or listening to this book outside, I welcome you to head out for the remainder of the chapter. Reduce the likelihood of any excuse to cut your wander short; leave your music and any other distractions behind, wear comfortable clothing, take along water, a snack, and a small blanket or towel to sit on. It might feel weird at first; where to go, what to do, how to feel. The beauty of forest bathing is how conducive to healing the practice is. Forest bathing allows us to relax and find comfort in nature and the opportunity to keep in touch with ourselves.

When alone, hold the vessel for yourself as you would when guiding participants.

A two-hour minimum seems to be the suggested practice standard in forest bathing, but even if you only have twenty or thirty minutes once a week, just go. Visit a location of your worksite you have never or rarely explored. Even spaces you've known for years can reveal new sensory delights. Or find a site that is far away from your place of work. Upon arrival, remember to congratulate yourself for taking this time for you. Forest bathing is a first step to incorporating sensory interpretation in your programs, providing opportunities to forge skills that elevate how you show up for your visitors.

Once at your location, relax into your sit spot. Move slowly through all your available senses:

**Close your eyes and inhale deeply. If you have your sense of smell, which smells of nature are landing with you?**

**If you are hearing-able, listen. What sounds near and far are arriving? Which sounds are natural, which are human made? If you are deaf, what ambiances, sensations, or vibrations are coming through?**

**If you have your sense of taste, breathe slowly through your mouth like you are gently sucking through a straw. What tastes are in the air?**

**If you are sight-able, open your eyes and notice something small in nature. If you are blind or low vision, wander with your cane or with a friend and find an object. How does it feel to the touch? Does it have a smell? If the object is safe to taste, what does it taste like?**

The following seven prompts can be used anytime you feel like forest bathing. They can also be printed and used as scrolls for invitations during forest bathing with others (see the first invitation called, "Find Your Spot" in Chapter 5). Perhaps you can work with what the land is offering the day you head out and create your own set of prompts to use.

What feature of this landscape is calling your attention the strongest?

_____

_____

_____

_____

_____

_____

_____

_____

_____

_____

_____

_____

How are you spending time with the more-than-human world in this very moment?

_____

_____

_____

_____

_____

_____

_____

_____

_____

_____

_____

_____

_____

_____

_____

What is soothing about nature today?

_____
_____
_____
_____
_____
_____
_____
_____
_____
_____
_____
_____
_____

What is something marvelous about nature you are experiencing here?

_____
_____
_____
_____
_____
_____
_____
_____
_____
_____
_____
_____
_____

Share a private thought with the trees around you.

_____
_____
_____
_____
_____
_____
_____
_____
_____
_____
_____
_____
_____
_____

Wander slowly and notice something small.

_____
_____
_____
_____
_____
_____
_____
_____
_____
_____
_____
_____
_____
_____

Which natural details are revealing themselves to you?

_____

_____

_____

_____

_____

_____

_____

_____

_____

_____

_____

_____

### Case Study: Explorations in Project Learning Tree from the Motor City

Saturday, April 1, 2023, was a great day to be an Alpha Kappa Alpha (AKA). The Enhance Our Environment Committee for AKA's Alpha Rho Omega of Detroit chapter, and Eta Iota Omega chapter based in Inkster, Michigan, helped foster a learning opportunity with the forestry division of the Michigan Department of Natural Resources through hosting a Project Learning Tree mini workshop for sorority members.

Alpha Kappa Alpha Sorority Incorporated® is one of the nation's largest Greek-letter organizations comprised of more than 355,000 initiated members in graduate and undergraduate chapters located in 12 countries. AKA is the first African American Sorority and has been active for 115 years, and ARO is the first AKA chapter in Michigan founded 100 years ago. It is the oldest Greek-letter organization established by African American college-educated women.

Many AKA chapter members are deeply involved with youth mentoring programs and PLT was the perfect professional development workshop to help bridge connections. AKA has developed a large catalog of programs encouraging life-long educational advancement in math, science, fellowships, and advocacy and it was a natural fit to share Project Learning Tree's award-winning, multi-sensory environmental education activities designed for teachers and other educators, parents, and community leaders to improve forest literacy for youth from preschool through grade 12.

A few participants arrived at the workshop with a natural fear of the outdoors but engaged fully with the sensory nature explorations of PLT. Activities provide participants with stimulating sensory engagement by collecting the colorful poker chips or pipe cleaners scattered throughout the room to demonstrate wildlife needs vs. availability of food, water, shelter, or touching the tree cookies and feeling the bark and growth rings learning how trees grow, or creating the sound of a thunderstorm through snapping, slapping, clapping, stomping. PLT activities helped make these connections between experiencing nature with the senses.

The following comments were shared by participants from their post-workshop feedback:

"I am a firm believer that the first step to enhancing our environment is through education and outreach as you can't enhance what you are unaware needs improvement. We look forward to taking back what we learned and implementing it among our community and upcoming tree plantings."

"I enjoyed the active participation, and the presenters were very energetic and engaging. Extremely knowledgeable and kept my interest. Well done!"

Participants were also asked to describe two ways they would apply what they learned today in their current career or role within their community. The answers suggested an interest in sharing time outdoors for health and wellness and happiness.

"Taking a break, maybe a walk outside."

"Show seniors how to plant trees; reintroduce them to the outdoors."

"I will use the activities to teach my students about interactions in nature. I will also use the information I received to give other educators tips and ideas to use in their classrooms."

"Encourage outside activities and understand the important role of our environment."

"I can use the information shared today with our Sustainability Committee at work."

"As a physician assistant professor, this could be translated to discuss cultural differences and implicit bias. I also like the tree planting activity."

Accolades to our Michigan Project Learning Tree Coordinator, Andrea Stay, for helping to put on a great educational workshop. I was elated to share this experience with both chapters of Alpha Kappa Alpha Sorority, Incorporated. Special shout-out to the Huron Pines AmeriCorps members who joined us.

Angel Squalls | Environmental Advocate and Project Manager

*"In the depth of winter, I finally learned that within me there lay an invincible summer."*
—Albert Camus

# Chapter 3

## REGENERATING A PROGRAMMING ETHOS

Do you remember the first time you discovered interpretation? Close your eyes and think back on the memory for a moment. Remember feeling that bolt of lightning inside when you found out you could make a living from it? Did you learn about interp as a child on vacation with your family? Was it during high school? College? Later in life? Guides similarly have their own unique stories of how, when, and where they first encountered forest bathing. A notable common denominator among guides is how serendipitous the timing was upon learning about the practice. I stumbled into forest bathing in 2019 in the wake of an interpretive program I implemented called *Women Managing Woodlands*. The program was the first of its kind held at the historic Oden State Fish Hatchery near Petoskey, Michigan, which occupies the ancestral, traditional, and contemporary lands of the Anishnaabek in the Lake Huron Watershed of the Northern Lower Peninsula. To launch the event, I recruited nine preeminent female conservationists from my state, and together we led visitors through the 130-acre parcel interpreting our knowledge and expertise of quality forest management.

They might seem like unconventional sites to interpret trees, but anyone who visits a Michigan state fish hatchery discovers an idyllic place for nature exploration. State fish hatcheries were established in the 1920s across Michigan through civilian labor and ingenuity. Our great-granddads—enabled by substantial support from their wives and moms—constructed buildings and outdoor rearing tanks to raise fish on small footprints of vast amounts of public land. These centennial projects created our six state fish hatcheries which collectively occupy incredibly diverse ecological landscapes, featuring hundreds of acres of non-industrial public forestland with trails, ponds, and an impressive array of biodiversity. Over time, Michigan's hatcheries have become treasured destinations explored and enjoyed by millions of national and international wanderers for far more than just the fish.

During our forestry program, we trekked the group beyond the sea of asphalt parking lots, driveways, and buildings, into the cool shade of upland hardwood communities, then past the outdoor exhibits descending to lowland coniferous swamps. As we wandered, we discussed diseases of trees as well as the value of harvests, vegetative plantings, unique habitats, and the wildlife communities dependent upon the successful implementation of these conservation practices. Although program participation stemmed from a genuine interest in dendrology, moving through the woods provoked measurable and

Subliminally discovering forest bathing while touring the grounds of the Oden State Fish Hatchery with *Women Managing Woodlands*, 2019

transformative impacts on mood. Program feedback echoed how much better participants "felt" after the hike. Several mentioned the delight of noticing ubiquitous plants and animals, most appreciated time spent outdoors, and one visitor revealed experiencing a deep calming feeling from moving through the woods with us.

Sometime later that season, I read the term, "forest bathing" in a *National Geographic* article and began discovering more and more references to the term. I found numerous essays and books written about the topic along with several online organizations that advocate the practice. From my research, I realized that our immersion in the woods at Oden was healing; lowering our blood pressure, increasing cerebral blood flow, lowering cortisol levels, alleviating environmental stressors, and making us feel good. I needed to learn more about this elysian magic.

Eventually I found the Association of Nature and Forest Therapy Guides and Programs (ANFT) and enrolled to become a certified forest therapy guide through ANFT. The only prerequisite of my certification training was to earn my Wilderness First Responder (WFR) certificate which I completed through the National Outdoor Leadership School (NOLS). My training cohort with ANFT was called "Silver Birch," and our online gatherings began January 9, 2021, three days after the deadly domestic insurrection to violently overthrow the United States government, destroy our democracy, and illegally install a deranged, criminal, psychopathic fever-brained despot through minority rule. All because a few dead slaveowners demanded an electoral college.

I arrived at our first Zoom class marinating in anger,

Celebrating my arrival at Walden Pond, October 2021. Concord, Massachusetts. *Photo by Andrea Z. Covey.*

51

disbelief, despair. But over the six-month course, I reconciled this grief using methods of forest bathing. The experience helped unlock an ability I'd desired for a dozen years: how to better harvest the benefits of nature using our available mammalian senses for delivering health, harmony, and peace. Upon completing the online coursework, I registered for part two of the training, an in-person follow-up that ANFT refers to as "Immersion." Although ANFT's Immersions are held all over the world, the Immersion I selected was called "Land of Thoreau" and took place in Lincoln, Massachusetts, the epicenter of the American Revolution. The purpose of Immersions are to deepen a guide's knowledge of the practice, witness guiding first hand from experienced trainers, and participate in face-to-face conversations to build community.

When I'm asked what I do as a forest bathing guide, I respond with a definition shared by my ANFT trainers: "I work in partnership with the more-than-human world, to accompany and support others on the journey through which they discover the whole of who they are." And what the heck does that mean? It means I guide mindfulness in nature, helping individuals remember or establish their own authentic relationships with nature using sensory invitations. Here the forest is the therapist, and the guide opens doors for participants.

During my certification coursework it grew increasingly clear that there were many undeniable correlations between guiding and interpreting, and learning the practice of guiding has profoundly enhanced my interpretative style. Whether considered a form of art or science—or both—guiding forest bathing provides me with specialized tools that improve experiences for my visitors and enhance my own personal enjoyment of my craft.

First, sensory practices have instilled a heightened level of engagement in our field. As outlined in his foreword to *Interpretation for the 21st Century, Fifteen Guiding Principles for Interpreting Nature and Culture, First Edition* (1997. Champaign, IL: Sagamore Publishing), interpreter and fellow Saluki Dr. Tim Merriman reminds us that "we must continue probing our profession for deeper understandings, principles learned from practice and new challenges. We must provoke ourselves to learn more in both familiar and unfamiliar settings." Forest bathing provides such occasions, motivating us to explore something new and harnessing the courage of taking on edgy challenges.

Another influence of forest bathing on my interpretive presentation is reminiscent of the perspective Sam Ham shared with us in his work, *Environmental Interpretation: A Practical Guide for People with Big Ideas and Small Budgets* (1992. Golden, CO: North American Press). "The best tours are dynamic. They don't merely consist of a series of stops in which the interpreter-guide stops the group and talks. Dynamic tours are more active, with each stop involving the audience in some exercise—intellectually, verbally, or physically." Ham continues, "Other possibilities are endless...using senses (smelling, listening, touching, etc.)...Involve the group in your tour." Forest bathing with visitors provides this next-level summit to my work. I engage visitors more effectively using movement and sensory explorations to tell the story, to make connections, to help my interpretive message stick. The standard sequence of forest bathing includes the very sensory invitations Ham refers to by creating dynamic programs over dull, robotic, rushed, or stale tours. At its root this approach means simplifying the experience. For example, if you deliver interpretive programs about {*insert natural resource here*}, how does that take shape? You marching a group to some observation platform, pointing at the scenery, regurgitating facts, taking questions, concluding your talk, listening to a soft chorus of tepid, lukewarm golf claps while thanking them for coming? Why not try something new?

Perhaps invite visitors to kick off their flip-flops and dip toes in some nearby surface water while you share information about the watershed. Or welcome guests to inhale slowly and notice the surrounding smells of the area while you discuss the resident wildlife. Or suggest visitors close their eyes and listen while describing how nature is landing with them using only one word, feel the smooth or rough stones you pass around when discussing area landforms, or taste a tea you've brewed from edible plants that grow underfoot in order that they may carry the essence of the landscape away within them. How else might you harness the senses with public outreach? The point is to leverage your interpretive talents by providing opportunities for deeper, holistic, more memorable sensory experiences for visitors employing more than backdrop and factoids of that same tired boiler-plate you've been using for years. Flip the script. Make the senses your new prop. As Tilden reminds us in his second principle of interpretation in *Interpreting Our Heritage, Third Edition* (1977. Chapel Hill, NC: The University of North Carolina Press), "Information, as such, is not Interpretation. Interpretation is revelation based upon information. But they are entirely different things…" Maybe it seems awkward or impossible to share sensory interpretation with bus groups of seventy-five who show up for your 2:00 p.m. tour—it isn't, just give it a try. If large groups seem too overwhelming, start with small ones. Bust out of your comfortable routine and challenge yourself. Stay curious. Take risks. Be your own change maker. The results can be remarkable.

Professor and interpretive author Dr. Doug Knapp preambles the absolute necessity of weaving the sensory concepts of forest bathing into interpretation in his book *Applied Interpretation, Putting Research into Practice* (2007. Fort Collins, CO: InterpPress). Here Knapp encourages readers to *be pragmatic*, "In sum, if I knew then what I know now, I would give my audience the experience of seeing a sunset from a ridge top rather than fill 40 minutes with ecological topics, human impacts on ecology, and ways to overcome global warming—which I did 20 years ago."

I've been guilty at mundane interp. I've led my share of tired programs and tours that fell flat. Sometimes my shortcomings stemmed from lazily leaning too heavily on nature "selling itself" without serving as the connective tissue between the resource and the visitor. Other times I oversold the beauty of nature, unnecessary excess Tilden refers to in *Interpreting Our Heritage*, as "that last tap," when too much pomp and pageantry deflect and detract your audience from the interpretive message. "Let us cultivate the power that lies in the understatement," advises Tilden.

While leading 4th grade classes down a nature trail—often sounding like a herd of elephants—my concerns over protecting the resource often curtailed the full embodiment of the interpretive experience I could have been providing them. So worried about some kid picking a flower, I never thought outside the box to have natural scents available to share, or to have us wander in silence and notice nature around us, or physically enact the flight of migrating geese. As a young interpreter, it never once dawned on me to have visiting schoolkids—or perhaps more importantly, their teachers—who were momentarily away from fluorescent lighting, poor indoor air quality, and the confining classroom, to pause quietly for a moment, lie down in the soft pine needles and gaze up at the forest canopy. Knapp expounds on this in *Applied Interpretation* by referring to interpretation as an "Episodic Event." "Whether we like it or not," Knapp explains, "the interpretive experience for an individual is a small blip on his or her life's radar. We have them for 30 to 40 minutes—maybe longer or shorter in some cases—and then they're gone."

Give yourself permission to shake things up and try a new approach now and again. Resuscitate that interpretive pioneer spirit. By applying the methods of forest bathing to your interpretive programs you'll increase the sum total of your interpretive game. As part of its strategic plan, the National Association for Interpretation (NAI) commenced the *Interpretation Standards Project* as a review of its national standards in 2016. Under the section entitled, *General Interpretation, Knowledge of Self,* the organization lists, "Be creative and open to trying something new" as the first quality of an interpreter's skills and abilities. NAI encourages this growth!

The sensory applications of forest bathing with visitors might not prove to be a monumental career-changer for every interpreter. However, it can help to restore a programming ethos by reigniting what Tilden called the "priceless ingredient." Guiding multi-sensory invitations is an effective workout to revive that enthusiasm and embodiment that led us to interpretation in the first place: deeply caring about the subject and about the visitor. The art and science of guiding sensory interpretation is a worthy endeavor, even it if is only a moment to feel peaceful and refreshed for a little while.

It might be a helpful exercise to differentiate the principles of guiding and interpretation.

## The Steep Unlearning Curve

With a film crew tagging along on his road trip from North Carolina to Philadelphia for the Mayflower Kennel Club Dog Show, champion bloodhound owner Harlan Pepper recalled his childhood habit of naming nuts and how it would infuriate his mom when she overheard him. "I used to be able to name every nut," Pepper reminisced for the camera, "peanut, hazelnut, cashew nut, Macadamia nut—that was the one that would send her into a...going crazy...she'd say, 'Harlan Pepper, you stop naming nuts!'"

Many of us fondly remember this hilarious scene from the 2000 comedy, *Best in Show*, directed by and starring Christopher Guest in the role of Harlan Pepper. I evoke the classic mockumentary as a fun way to remember that forest bathing also invites us to stop naming nuts—and all other flora and fauna for that matter. And this is one significant difference between guiding and interpreting.

During forest bathing programs some guides will suggest that participants try and quell the temptation of identifying trees, plants, or wildlife while silently moving through the woods. It's challenging for many of us to turn off our inner-naturalist's voice, but it's important to remember because the ultimate purpose of forest bathing is to get out of our heads and back into our bodies using sensory, not intellectual explorations. This coincides with reflections from Enos Mills in his book *The Adventures of a Nature Guide* (1923. Garden City, NY: Doubleday, Page & Co.). "To have made friends with one tree, is better than to have learned the names of many trees." While forest bathing, we are not concerned with expanding our bird life lists. There is no "destination." We are not out there to get our steps in. Rather, the intention is to spend time in the woods, moving slowly, using all available senses to nurture mindfulness in nature. As guides, we are taking people on little journeys to embody wholeness through a transient, relaxed state of mind.

Another fundamental distinction between interpretation and forest bathing is that when guiding, we are not looking for outcomes. ANFT founder and trainer Amos Clifford reminds us that forest bathing focuses on the here and now (not the there and then). While interpreters commonly write objectives and seek outcomes for programs and events, the point of guiding forest bathing programs is to let go of expectations and allow participants to experience their own unique connections with nature, enabling them to control what they feel. This is not to say we don't want, seek, or benefit from post-bathing feedback, because we do. But the steep unlearning curve for interpreters surrenders our attachment to the outcome of a program.

Forest bathing guides don't prescribe, promise, set expectations, set goals, determine outcomes, diagnose, psychoanalyze, intellectualize, project, force, pressure, judge, heal, or teach. We don't over-acknowledge or affirm participant's emotional responses or reactions during group sharing times following each invitation. Interpreters may find this mannerism incredibly challenging because we are used to affirming visitors' dialogue to demonstrate engagement and opportunities for learning and sharing, but when guiding we are not setting goals or seeking outcomes, we offer choice and create the space for everyone to exist. Douglas Knudson, Ted Cable, and Larry Beck foreshadow this idea in their work, *Interpretation of Cultural and Natural Resources, Second Edition* (2003. State College, PA: Venture Publishing Inc.). "Know when to be quiet. While observing wildlife, a spectacular overview, a sunset, or a moonrise, or a dramatic piece of art, silence is appropriate. Let the visitors experience the moment in peace. They do not need to hear that it looks beautiful, cool, or awesome." The same is true if and when participants choose to share their thoughts after invitations during forest bathing. As a guide, it's unnecessary to say anything after the participants except "*thank you*" as you move along the circle. We avoid making comments after they share, because we really want people to have the space to be totally free to do what they

Regenerating a Programming Ethos

want and feel how they want to. There is no need to overcompensate. Guides want to honor all stories without trying to top them.

Guiding aligns with a wild tending ethic where all non-human creatures are kin, and we maintain a reciprocal relationship. Guiding rejects a "leave no trace" mindset which infers separation from nature, a look but don't touch attitude.

Guides invite sensory connections, work in partnership with nature and the land, open doors, offer hospitality, offer invitations, witness, work in liminality, accompany, use a standard sequence, uphold professional standards, and we know how to go with the flow.

## Compatible Archetypes

The good news is that when it comes to guiding, interpreters possess several occupational advantages. So many of an interpreter's inherent qualities are naturally suited to forest bathing because guiding requires skills intuitively available in our wheelhouse. Guides and interpreters open doors to discovery of the natural world. Both foster relationships between participants and the outdoors. Both share invitations for connections in nature.

Interpreters don't guess, dismiss, argue, interrupt, ignore, mock, disrespect, or deceive. And we avoid all of this because we really want to provide visitors with a meaningful message that provokes instead of repels.

Interpreters listen, engage, create, welcome, celebrate, research, adapt, make goals, develop, design, implement, evaluate, and we know how to read a room.

Parallels linking guiding and interpreting also incorporate nature exploration for the sake of protecting the resource. As young interpreters we all learn Tilden's mantra, "Through interpretation, understanding; through understanding, appreciation; through appreciation, protection." Guides also work in partnership with the more-than-human world and the land, embodying a kin-centric world view, adopting a reciprocal mindset, and nurturing deeper curiosity about the forest in order to become stewards of the land.

The art of hospitality at the beginning and end of all programs is a similar ritual for guides and interpreters. Hospitality is nothing less than creating an atmosphere that makes participants feel welcomed and assuring them that they've arrived at a safe space. This along with an omni-partial view of participants, treating all guests equally and fairly, remains the same to both disciplines. Beck and Cable refer to this as "meeting the needs of the whole person."

Modeling ease is another custom shared by guides and interpreters. Whether it's a rambunctious kid on a program, a visitor questioning your message, or trauma emerging while forest bathing, the role of guides and interpreters is to stay calm—stay focused. It's challenging, but through experience we understand how to keep cool and roll with it under stressful encounters, and it serves our trades well.

## Attracting New Communities

The very nature of forest bathing invites new communities to our sites. Forest bathing provides a platform to tweak language and technique based on what the guide is passionate about, what it is they want to do, how far they want to take the practice, and how much they want to learn and grow in guiding. Forest bathing reflects an adaptable approach where interpreters stand to expand their audiences once adopting it and offering it as a reoccurring part of their annual community programming.

Since my first encounter with forest bathing, I guide sensory interpretive programs regularly at the Oden State Fish Hatchery, various Michigan state parks, and other publicly owned venues across the State of Michigan as an effort to reach visitors and inspire anyone to try guiding. It's a tough job, but somebody's got to do it. I offer forest bathing for groups that I never previously considered partnering with and influential organizations with forward-thinking leaders who are discovering the value of forest bathing for their members. One unique opportunity materialized when the Michigan Science Teachers Association (MSTA) invited me to present at their 70th Annual Conference in 2023. The opportunity enabled Michigan teachers to experience

Guiding my first forest bathing wander, Cheboygan State Park, Michigan, 2021. *Photo by Shari Nelson.*

forest bathing—many for the first time. I shared ideas for teachers to incorporate sensory discoveries into lesson plans as a fresh, innovative means to reach students across a spectrum of subjects.

University of Michigan psychology researchers, Marc Berman, John Jonides, and Stephen Kaplan discovered that after spending one hour outdoors in nature, people experienced a 20% increase in memory and attention span. Incorporating forest bathing outings into semester curriculum can make a positive difference on student performance and mood.

Sharing Forest Bathing with Michigan Teachers, MSTA 2023.

Another meaningful partnership I treasure is with Opportunities Unlimited for the Blind in Michigan (OUB), an organization dedicated to building skills and community with blind and low-vision children. Working together with the community of OUB yielded mutually beneficial impacts using multi-sensory nature explorations. It provided me with a deeper mindfulness of sensory applications in guiding and interpreting. From time spent with the organization, I became a better park interpreter through observation, listening, adjusting technique, letting go, welcoming whatever arrives, and embracing a multi-sensory approach to nature exploration. My creativity skyrocketed and the partnership revitalized my interpretive approach. Forest bathing with blind campers continues to steer me towards interpretive excellence, using mindfulness of language, applying new methods to create mindfulness in nature for inspiring young people, and reveling in the joy from their inspiration.

Forest bathing also lends itself to working with communities where English is a second language. I've guided children and families of

Sensory Interpretation with Opportunities Unlimited for the Blind.

nonprofit organizations working to provide essential human resources for migrant, immigrant, and refugee families. Multi-sensory journeys transcend language barriers and provide interpreters and guides with deeply meaningful experiences supporting historically underserved, marginalized communities.

In the September/October 2018 issue of *Legacy*, our NAI legend, the late Will LaPage, tests our grit in his essay, *The Complete Interpreter: The Limits of Our Beliefs*. There he wrote, "By choosing to be in the game, we not only interpret to those who come to us, we also search out new audiences." LaPage continued, "If we believe that our heritage is worth preserving, can we really afford to stay out of the game, staying on the sidelines and hoping that others will champion our cause?"

Think of new audiences you have never worked with to share sensory interpretation through forest bathing.

## The Long Arc of Our Mentors

The outstanding thing about our chosen profession is that we are led by many who are committed to uplifting us. We are continually being encouraged by contemporary industry leaders to try new things and they've been beating this drum for decades. It's helpful to know that around every bend we find enthusiastic encouragement to step out of our comfort zone and take a leap of faith when it calls. At any rate, how awesome it is that we are never without our own personal cheering section?

In her book, *Inspired to Inspire* (2021. Calgary, CA: Tortuga Creative Studio), author Jacquie Gilson poses the question, "Is it the job of an interpreter to remind people to stop and smell the flowers and reflect on their beauty and utility?" Gilson goes on to answer her question in the affirmative, reminding us that visitors arrive at our sites—places away from their home and work—precisely for the element of escape and it makes perfect sense to take advantage of the chance to offer them moments during their visits to pause, relax, unwind, recharge. Gilson developed the *Holistic Inspirational Interpretation* concept which, in small part, views people as "whole beings…with different entry points for inspiration." Holistic Inspirational Interpretation further suggests that reaching visitors first on an emotional level opens the doors for cognitive remembrance (this sounds familiar). Forest bathing with visitors categorically enables these connections.

"Everyone can be creative," noted authors Lisa Brochu and Tim Merriman in their work, *Personal Interpretation, Connecting Your Audience to Heritage Resources, Third Edition* (2015. Fort Collins, CO: InterpPress), "even though some people tend to allow their right brains to get a little lazy from time to time. After all, it's usually easier to follow a formula than come up with something different or new. Nevertheless, it is possible to cultivate your creative side. You simply have to exercise it, just like an unused muscle."

"Constant innovation" is what Douglas Knudson, Ted Cable, and Larry Beck remind us of in their book, *Interpretation of Cultural and Natural Resources, Second Edition* (2003. State College, PA: Venture Publishing Inc.). "Successful interpretation requires innovation. Sites that have had the same displays exhibited for decades or have been offering the same old programs may be neither successfully fulfilling their mission nor garnering much public support."

Beyond these endorsements for professional advancement, evident too is the historically persistent and recurring theme from our mentors embracing sensory exploration in interpretation.

In Grant W. Shape's work, *Interpreting the Environment, Second Edition* (1976. Seattle, WA: John Wiley & Sons), contributing author Paul H. Risk addresses the technique of using all the senses. "Most interpretation takes advantage only of sight and hearing. Visitors stand looking at a particular view or object while the interpreter explains it. Show and tell! The enlarging of one's environmental awareness through extended use of the senses is limitless."

Larry Beck and Ted Cable refer to "Presenting a Multi-sensory Whole" in *Interpretation for the 21st Century, Second Edition*. "Engaging as many of the visitors' senses as possible allows the interpreter to go beyond meeting intellectual needs alone. Touching, seeing, smelling, tasting, and listening all help communicate as a whole... Activating the senses creates a holistic experience for people."

The long arc of our mentors bends towards our successes.

## In a "Nutshell"

It's important to stress that this book is in no way an invitation to compare and despair. Interpreters should adopt personal interpretation that makes sense for their missions, their sites, their visitors, and importantly, themselves.

There's no shame in offering the same interpretive programs for twenty years; often that's precisely how expertise is born and thrives. In fact, you may be offering programs that fellow interpreters have learned from you and have adopted at their own sites, thereby spreading the wealth of your interpretive repertoire and elevating your colleagues. If visitors keep flocking to your signature programs year after year, that speaks volumes to their impact and your success. But some of us arrive at a point in our career where we feel underwhelmed, uninspired, or even bored; some fervently searching for new ideas to boost an existing interpretive catalog.

Whether you are a new interpreter, a seasoned interpreter, or a semi-retired interpreter, forest bathing with visitors can help stoke that fire inside that got us interested in interpretation in the first place. Through leaning in and trying this, you'll nurture the triple bottom line benefiting self, site, society. At a minimum weaving the sensory elements of forest bathing into the mix offers interpreters a fresh, restorative opportunity to explore and rediscover their sites by experiencing a deeper connection in nature and leading by inspiration. At best, applying sensory interpretation provides professionals with the ability to invigorate our core purpose of enriching visitor experiences.

It turns out that forest bathing is demonstrably compatible with our interpretive DNA. Although there are slight adjustments to be made in our mannerisms, new approaches to learn, and occupational habits to tame, adopting this practice is an easy layup. Additionally, doing so provides interpreters with challenges to expand our reach, melding familiar talents with an unfamiliar practice.

As guides and interpreters, we are rooted in what brought us to these professions; we are intentional in purpose and seek to establish a baseline proficiency in our respected practices to grow in our work. We bring our personal life experiences, our stories, and our own unique creativity to shape and share our passions. It is our pedigree.

What is your interpretive programming ethos and how might the methods of forest bathing advance your professional growth?

## Case Study—Sensing a Wonderous Tree

One of my all-time favorite nature programs combined multi-sensory experiential learning with a powerful environmental message. For summer campers at the Marine Science Institute in Redwood City, California, a field trip to Pescadero State Beach provided a fun opportunity to explore a variety of habitats near the ocean. Among these were the salt marsh and upland woods surrounding it. Camp instructors and counselors would lead their groups of young naturalists along a sandy trail, winding through marsh grasses, scrub brush, and eventually into a sparse grove of trees.

Throughout the journey, campers were encouraged to take note of all the different sounds, smells, and sights they encountered. What did the air sound and smell like, blowing through the marsh off the ocean? How many different birds and insects did they see and hear moving from tree to tree? How many great blue herons could they spot hanging out near their rookery? How about egrets, snowy and great? Did they smell the different plants to help identify them? How did the sounds and smells change as they moved out of the marsh and into the woods?

This nature walk culminated at one of the most memorable trees I have ever visited: a grand, old, sprawling eucalyptus tree.

Its lateral spread and perfectly forked vertical trunks provided welcome shade from the summer sun and more than enough child-sized perches for our group of campers. Within its tangled web of branches, they each found their own sitting place as instructors encouraged them to examine their amazing host: put your ear up to the smooth bark—can you hear the water flowing inside? What does it feel like? Smell like? How does the sunlight change as it filters through the leaves?

Filled with curiosity and appreciation for this wondrous tree, the campers were asked to close their eyes and just listen. Seated below them, an instructor would break out a well-worn copy of *The Lorax* by Dr. Seuss and softly read it aloud to the group. With the audience quite literally immersed in the tree, it is hard to imagine a more fitting setting to deliver the book's memorable conservation message.

Terri Teller | Forest Ranger with the State of Maine Forest Service

"*Without leaps of imagination or dreaming, we lose the excitement of possibilities. Dreaming, after all is a form of planning.*"
—Gloria Steinem

# Chapter 4

---

## PLANNING TO BATHE

In the fall of 1997, I was enrolled in Dr. Cem Basman's Forestry 391 Resources course at Southern Illinois University (SIU), and Professor Basman kicked off our semester by assigning some warm-up planning exercises to ease into our new semester. It seems incredible to me now, but he was the first teacher I ever had to suggest that we work with fellow students we'd never previously partnered with—break momentarily from our comfortable factions and team up with classmates who we barely knew to break barriers and practice personable, social skill sets—a prodigious exercise necessary for developing those fluid professional mannerisms we'd be needing for entering the workforce ahead.

He left our assemblage to us, and it took no time to wander the room and introduce ourselves to unfamiliar classmates. Dr. Basman then informed us we would be delivering group presentations about meeting and interviewing someone salient in Carbondale. This work triggered us to pay attention, to tune in, to "notice" our surroundings and take stock in that person, revealing their value in our community to the class.

Our next preliminary assignment involved trying something new (so long as it was moral and legal), followed by eating something new (same guidelines). We experienced challenging and critical lessons in this resource management course as the semester progressed, but these initial icebreakers laid our foundation of learning to coordinate, to communicate, to strategize—to plan. It was also around this same time that Dr. Basman helped us navigate the formation of a student

My SIU forestry professors, circa 1998. Dr. Cem Basman, center. Questions?

chapter of the National Association for Interpretation at SIU in order that we flourish and thrive in our first shared professional community.

This resource class along with other experiences sparked an interest within me to broaden my foundational knowledge of the management of natural resources. To meet that goal, I served for many years as a professional conservation planner for the United States Department of Agriculture's Nature Resources Conservation Service (NRCS). The agency is rooted in its planning mission of the "Nine Steps of Conservation Planning." These steps help land managers address natural resource concerns of SWAPA+H (soil, water, air, plants, animals, and the human impacts of planning) on private land and offer alternative solutions to landowners addressing those concerns.

An additional purpose of the steps is to develop and implement plans that protect, conserve, and enhance natural resources within a social and economic prospective. In a planning course I attended, trainer and USDA Resource Conservationist Sally Van Lieu offered a lighthearted insight: "You can apply the nine steps of conservation planning to other areas of your life, professional and personal." Lieu continued, "A very good friend had a personal problem she was struggling with, so over a couple of beers, I talked her through the steps, and it worked. Learning how to move strategically forward with a plan helped resolve her issue."

Sometimes it's hard to know where to start when adopting a new interpretive program, activity, or event. Here are the adulterated USDA's Nine Steps of Conservation Planning which may serve useful when planning forest bathing programs for visitors.

## Identify Opportunities, Determine Objectives, Inventory Resources

With these steps, appropriate social and economic resources for the plan are harvested. It is important that as much information as possible can be collected so that the plan will fit the needs of everyone involved. Is your interpretive networking outreach organized? Do you have the ability to market the program using your employer's resources or a local source? Do you have funding to offer forest bathing? Do you have a trail or another outdoor space to use? Do you have a dependable network that would enjoy watching you meld your interpretive talents with forest bathing? Does your community have an interest in forest bathing?

## Analyze Resource Data

Study your available resources and clearly define existing conditions for all of the interpretive programming, including limitations and potential for desired expansion. For example, would forest bathing be a one-and-done or do you have resources to try offering a series of opportunities? This step is crucial to developing forest bathing programs that will work for your visitors and your site. It also provides a clear understanding of the baseline conditions that will help to judge how effective a program is after it has been put into place.

## Formulate Alternatives

Alternatives are ideas or plans. The purpose of this step is to achieve the goals for the plan, by solving all identified problems (lack of funding, lack of community awareness surrounding forest bathing, a boss that needs convincing), taking advantage of opportunities (grant opportunities, marketing efforts through partnerships, selling forest bathing's potential to leadership), and meeting the social, economic, and environmental needs of the planning project. For example, decide on multiple options for offering forest bathing on- and off-site. Consider conferences or existing community partner events. Often this step can help formulate funding or planning alternatives that help offset the financial expense of implementing plans.

### Evaluate Alternatives

Evaluate the alternatives to determine their effectiveness in addressing the visitor experience, opportunities, and objectives by introducing a forest bathing program into your current suite of programs. Identify the strengths and weaknesses of your plan.

### Make Decisions

At this point the interpreter chooses if the new forest bathing program will work best for their situation. In the case of broad-reaching interpretive plans, input from colleagues or a public review and comment may be obtained before a decision is reached.

### Implement the Plan

Technical assistance should be sought to help with implementing professionally designed interpretive plans. Seek available assistance in developing the final plans, and assessments for available trails, parking lots, bathroom facilities, then mobilize your efforts and implement a forest bathing program.

### Evaluate the Plan

How did it go? Is there a demand for more? Interpretive planning is an ongoing process that continues long after the implementation of a program or project. By evaluating the effectiveness of an interpretive plan or a practice within a plan, one can decide whether to continue with other aspects of an overall programming-wide strategy.

## So What?

The theme of this chapter is how to plan a forest bathing experience for your visitors. Until now, we have touched on planning basics broadly, but let's narrow our focus now on personal interpretive planning and how that relates to guiding forest bathing. And no discussion on personal interpretation would be complete without a review of the premiere foundational works of the interpretive approach to communication.

Developed by Dr. Sam Ham, professor emeritus with the University of Idaho, the interpretive approach to communication resulted from decades of extensive research of many different branches of psychology and social psychology relating to how people respond to persuasive communications. Through the breadth of his work, Ham revealed two important lessons for interpreters to learn and use to achieve successful communication. The first lesson is ensuring that communication will attract and keep the attention of an audience long enough to deliver a point, and the second lesson is that communication makes the point in a compelling way. Both lessons are needed to be successful at interpretation. From this, Ham created the EROT framework: which means that interpretation should be Enjoyable, Relevant, Organized and Thematic.

These abbreviations represent four qualities needed to achieve the two original lessons, and the framework was an evolutionary process. Initially, Ham recognized that keeping the audience entertained and engaged was of the utmost importance to interpretive success, because if you lose their attention, no message will stick. As such, ERO was created first. Later it made more sense to ensure that an interpretive message is in fact delivered. Therefore the 'T' was added. Ham introduced the world to EROT through his 1992 book, *Environmental Interpretation: A Practical Guide for People with Big Ideas and Small Budgets* (1992. Golden, CO: North American Press).

By 1998, Ham reordered the EROT framework and created the TORE model of thematic communication in order that the *T* should be first and foremost in an interpretive communication strategy. With the emphasis on Theme, ORE has lesser bearing aside from keeping an audience entertained. "When the T is added at the front," shared Ham, "the interpreter's attention is focused on how to apply ORE in a purposeful and strategic way."

Since the mid-1980s, Ham has delivered dozens of university classes, workshops, and research symposia on the TORE model in nearly fifty countries. The TORE model was the first and currently remains the only empirically substantiated applied communication model ever to be published specifically for interpreters. In 2013, Ham published *Interpretation: Making a Difference on Purpose* (2013. Golden, CO: Fulcrum Books), which reviewed a brief history of the EROT framework that led to the TORE model and how this defining framework inspired other interpretive industry leaders to utilize and endorse the framework towards best practices in our field.

In 2000, when Lisa Brochu and Tim Merriman created NAI's Certified Interpretive Guide (CIG) curriculum, they looked to incorporate fundamental resources from interpretive leaders like Dr. Ham. Brochu and Merriman wanted to highlight the value of the work of interpretation through measurable objectives, so with consent, they added the *P* for *Purposeful* and modified Ham's original TORE model into a new acronym, PEROT. Some years after the CIG curriculum was in use, CIG trainer Patti "Wren" Smith approached Brochu and Merriman about adding a *Y* to the acronym to represent *You*. The *You* indicates the importance of our professional interpretive growth and ability to adapt to audiences and circumstances throughout our careers. The acronym was reordered into "P.O.E.T.R.Y."

The first trial run of a CIG workshop took place in La Paz, Mexico, in December 2000, followed by the first ever Certified Interpretive Trainer workshop in Fort Collins, Colorado, in January 2001. For the next eleven years, Brochu and Merriman continually revised and modified the CIG curriculum based upon feedback and suggestions to "keep content current, relevant and responsive to field practitioners," as stated by Brochu. "In that sense, every person we trained as trainers had a hand in shaping the curriculum."

Let's review P.O.E.T.R.Y. and compare how it relates to developing personal interpretation of a forest bathing program for visitors.

**Interpretation serves a Purpose: The program can and should support the mission and goals of the organization.**

If the mission and goals are to provide enriching experiences for visitors, introducing forest bathing is an ideal way to explore the site. Forest bathing programs draw in new audiences and offer a unique sensory experience for visitors. The impacts of forest bathing programs on visitors most often result in a heightened appreciation for the land and renewed interest in protection of the resource. This reaction can manifest in increased community buzz, donations, or other contributions.

**Interpretation is Organized: Interpretation is organized when it is easy to process and follow without getting lost or overwhelmed.**

The standard sequence of forest bathing designed by ANFT follows a natural flow. We guide in three phases which includes, the "way in" to the forest, called Threshold of Connection. The second phase is liminality, an experience between space and time, and the final phase which provides the way out of the forest, back to the tamed world, which is called Threshold of Incorporation. Within those three phases are the sequence of Hospitality, Introductions, Pleasures of Presence, What's in Motion, Invitations, Tea Ceremony. Using this standard sequence provides a balanced combination of structure and predictability for the audience, which enables trust, and provides plenty of room for the guide's creativity and adaptation to circumstances. Forest bathing is also organized in terms of the anatomy of the sequence. It has a comprehensible flow.

**Interpretation is Enjoyable: People participate in interpretive programs because they want to, not because they have to, so they expect to enjoy themselves.**

The characteristics of forest bathing lend themselves to a heightened level of engagement with your visitors. Guides themselves should feel recharged at the conclusion of a forest bathing program. If guides feel tired or strained, it's a likely indication that they are getting too involved in the outcome or experience of visitors. Visitors who experience being guided will experience a program that invites them to momentarily let go and relax, taking in nature using their senses. The premise is about choice and being in the moment—not having to do anything more than be there—which is why as guides we start each invitation by letting the visitors know that the act of merely showing up speaks volumes and is enough.

**Interpretation is Thematic: A strong theme provides a platform for audiences to think their own thoughts and make their own meaning.**

One theme of forest bathing is personal wellness and renewal. The very essence of offering "invitations" to participants while guiding forest bathing is that there is no wrong way to do an invitation. Guides don't control. Our role is to allow space for people to have their own experience. Participants choose to do or not do whatever they feel like during forest bathing.

**Interpretation is Relevant: People pay attention to and respond to things that matter to them.**

The focus of forest bathing is "noticing." Slowing down in nature to notice things our gaze is drawn to. The purpose of forest bathing is paying attention and noticing how nature lands within us. Visitors will respond to the opportunity to reconnect with nature in this quiet method.

**You make the difference: Your passion and individual style can make the difference in how audiences respond.**

When learning to guide, think of your style regarding invitations and overall program delivery. Some guides offer very long-stretched wordy invitations, others offer the bare bones. Find your style and continue to mold and shape it with every guiding experience.

## Preparing to Guide a Forest Bathing Event

Planning is critical to the success of any meaningful work. There are many considerations when planning a forest bathing event for the public. The following outline can serve as a helpful tool:

<u>Sixteen weeks before the event:</u>

Decide upon your target audience. Do you want to offer forest bathing for adults only, kids only, or both? It's an important first step to consider because knowing who you will be sharing the practice with helps fine-tune language, style, invitations, and duration of program. It also helps avoid confusion or disappointment. If a family shows up to an adults-only program, they might be bummed there are no other families there to connect with. Conversely, if an individual adult arrives at a kid-friendly program, they might feel out of place or even distracted by the energy of the young humans.

Decide upon your time frame: morning, afternoon, or evening?

No trail is perfect but locate one that meets as many needs as possible including parking options, restroom availability, site conditions, and human foot traffic. Begin a conversation with the agency, organization, or individual that owns the land about using it for a public forest bathing program.

Continue practicing the standard sequence to grow comfortable with the phases and invitations (see the ANFT Standard Sequence outlined in Chapter 1 under "The Journey of Forest Bathing").

Twelve weeks before the event:

Begin marketing with details of date, time, location, what to bring, appropriate age level, registration/payment forms.

Begin gathering program supplies (see Additional Resources list following the Appendix).

If you're planning a cold-weather event and intend to use a fire, check with the property manager, and follow local fire ordinances to ensure a safe experience.

Plan refreshments (tea, dried or fresh fruit, etc.). Consider avoiding snacks with nuts or other food allergens.

If you're a free-radical like me, research state laws and prepare liability waiver forms for participants. Acorn Programs (www.acornprograms .com) offers courses on Professional Development that cover ideas on liability and insurance.

Practice your talk and your timing.

Two weeks before the event:

Double check that trail. Scout it out for obstructions or any safety concerns including trip hazards or overhead hanging dead branches or snags. Take a good look around the landscape.

One week before the event:

Reach out to participants to remind them about program date, time, location, items they should bring, and other hospitality details including any parking or restroom information.

Prepare program supplies including scrolls for the "Find Your Spot" invitation. (If you plan to offer this invitation, see the prompts at the end of Chapter 2 for scroll language ideas.)

Keep an eye on the weather for severe weather alerts or fire safety concerns if you plan to have a campfire.

One day before the event:

Re-scout the area and forest canopy for safety and pinpointing program stops.

Inventory and pack up all program supplies.

## Two hours before the event:
Heat water for tea, keep it in reliable portable thermos, pack up cups and thermos. Double check that you have all the supplies you need.

## One hour before the event:
Arrive early to set up props you plan to use. While you are doing this you can simultaneously scout the site for safety.

Put up directional road signs to the parking area if necessary. They are often necessary.

Place small yard signs or sandwich board signs at the trailhead to let public visitors that are not with your forest bathing group know that silence is appreciated.

## After the event:
Touch base with everyone through text, email, or tagging them on social media. Share photos and gratitude. Invite follow-up questions. Stay in touch.

## Leaning into Edges
Edges are feelings that range from mildly to radically uncomfortable. Forest bathing participants can have edges during invitations from just entering a forest, insecurity over their own mobility while moving through the woods, being around strangers in a program, or being invited to close their eyes, sit or lie down on the forest floor, share what they are noticing with the group after invitations, or even drinking tea at the program's conclusion.

Facing our edges is another benefit of forest bathing. Author and physician Dr. Suzanne Bartlett Hackenmiller interprets the concept of edges in her work, *The Outdoor Adventurer's Guide to Forest Bathing: Using Shinrin-Yoku to Hike, Bike, Paddle, and Climb Your Way to Health and Happiness* (2019. Lanham, MD: Falcon Guides). One goal she highlights with forest bathing is "to bring each participant to the edge of his or her comfort zone." Hackenmiller reminds us that edges are different for each person, whether it involves uncomfortableness with taking shoes off during a program or closing one's eyes during an invitation. "The recommendation is to simply observe that edge, attempting not to judge or fear it, recognizing that everyone experiences it in different ways." The belief is that when we step out of our comfort zone and teeter on those edges, a return on personal growth is yielded in several areas. Recognizing our edges helps shape mental resiliency.

Edges can also be felt by forest bathing guides themselves when experiencing the uncertainty of meeting new participants, the immense responsibly of group safety, perceived dangers along the forested trails such as moving around dead snags that could fall during a program, and looming foul weather threats. We also feel an edge when we learn of other certified forest bathing guides in our regions. A guide might worry about losing their audience to other guides or losing the uniqueness of their own guiding style.

Safety is always paramount to our work as interpreters and as guides. Always scout the landscape before the program begins to ensure obstacles are removed or at least identified. Always share "awareness" with the group prior to moving down the trail to make participants aware of poison ivy, the presence of ticks, or avoiding trip hazards like slippery rocks or exposed tree roots. Consider having participants sign a liability waiver ahead of a forest bathing program. By reviewing the awareness with your audience, it helps reinforce a sense of security for your participants, and assurance that they have arrived in a safe place and serves as the ultimate "heads-up." More importantly, sharing awareness tells your guests that you care about them, they are in good company, and you've got them covered.

Interpretive moments such as wildlife sightings occurring during programs are an interpreter's dream. However, if for example a bird flies by or calls while you are together in a sharing circle while forest bathing, they will most certainly distract the group. Now I can already hear the grumbling, but when someone is sharing something deep or profound with the group and an owl flies by or a fox runs down the path it becomes a delicate challenge to refocus the group's attention to the person who was speaking. Worse, if a puppy makes an appearance, forget it. You've lost the group and are now at the mercy of the owner for how long this adorable distraction lasts. When animals emerge during forest bathing, don't channel your inner Hermione Granger; don't share the Latin name, don't discuss the habitat, don't relay the life history, don't overreact to puppy mojo. Model ease, pause briefly, and redirect the group's attention to the sharing circle. Remember we are forest bathing to get out of our heads and back into our bodies. The idea is not to interpret the owl but explore how the owl makes you feel.

Over-talkers can be a struggle, especially when forest bathing in the winter. If you have one on your program, suggest that folks limit their sharing to one word, or one sentence.

And for that matter, weather can be a distraction for obvious reasons. Heat, cold, rain, snow, and wind all impact the natural serenity of forest bathing in one way or another. Guides do their best to prepare their participants beforehand and to go with the flow and model ease.

I remember beginning the somatics of moving people through Pleasures of Presence, inviting folks who cared to, to close their eyes or soften their gaze as we fully "arrived in the forest." Having participants notice the smells, tastes, then sounds of nature—and then the peace suddenly broken by three cackling people not with our group, growing louder and louder as they moved up the trail towards us. We learned all about their grocery store incident and how rude the cashier was to one of them and how they are never going back to that store again!

I reacted by pausing the activity and asked everyone to breathe quietly until the gaggle passed; once peace returned, we resumed the experience.

There is never a perfect trail. Anticipate disruptions. When they

happen, model ease and go with the flow. Participants will often look to the guide to determine how to react. If you allow distractions and disturbances to roll off you, it's very likely your participants will respond similarly.

Loud visitors during Pleasures of Presence can be particularly disruptive. As a guide, you can help alleviate this issue by placing metal pronged yard signs or sandwich board signs up in prominent locations prior to the start of the program, to caution visitors not with your group to be aware of the program ahead.

One step I always take during "Hospitality" at the start of forest bathing is to share an important awareness, to inform the group that we could in fact run into people on public trails that are not with our group and that if that happens, we will ignore them like passing spirits. Often this does the trick because if and when we are disrupted by an approaching unleashed dog or loud people, the group was made aware of that possibility ahead of time and accepts the momentary interruption.

I also make sure to discuss weather. How to react to inclement weather, what we do if it really downpours, what the plan is. I offer participants the opportunity to leave the program if it is too edgy for them to be in the rain. I ask that they let me know if they have to leave so that I'm not worried about their safety or whereabouts later.

Guiding is a funky juggling act, especially if you are an interpreter by trade. Balancing group dynamics while rejecting concern for the outcome, welcoming all stories, demonstrating indifference to sharing to avoid demonstrating favoritism or bias, not controlling the outcome but trying to lay down awareness. … It's not always easy but if you are prepared by making your group aware of potential interruptions, then when they happen, it's not as big of a deal.

## The Noise of Humanity

An old college buddy of mine manages the interpretive program for a large midwestern park and recently shared their feelings about implementing a forest bathing experience at their site: "I have thought of doing a forest bathing program here, but with 2.5 million visitors I am afraid I do not have a quiet or peaceful area of woods for this type of programming unless it falls in winter." <Sad trombone>.

Fortunately, seasonal visitor drop-offs hold no bearing on forest bathing. Besides, 2.5 million visitors are not all showing up on the same day, those are annual totals. As amazing as it sounds, forest bathing does not require the event to be held on an uninhabited island. Of course, we would all love an escape like that, but here we are among one another, and experienced guides learn to use what the land is offering, even if that includes the indelible noise of *us*. I understand the seasonal planning misconceptions when it comes to forest bathing, but the practice carries particularly valuable benefits for the urbanites (a club I was born into). In my experience, the more populated the area, the greater the interest, no matter the season.

Amidst skepticism, there are many direct and indirect management techniques interpreters can use to offer a quieter forest bathing experience for fair-weather crowds; adjust the program timing. Offer early-bird bathing, or a moonlight meander. Plan other events or programs in places away from the forest bathing area to siphon off some of the crowd. Close or redirect a trail you would like to use. Or pick a day and place and just go for it because the ideal time for forest bathing is here and now. Season and space are non-factors, whether you live in Honolulu, Hawaii, or Yellowknife, Canada; Tokyo, Japan, or Pocatello, Idaho; whether your site is a half-acre lot or millions of acres. Some guides have offered summer forest bathing under a single tree in Central Park, NYC. Don't cop out and prevent innovative public programming over empty fears of our human racket.

It's important to welcome voices on this topic from professionals guiding forest bathing within our planet's largest metropolises:

## Mindful Nature Guide, Jill Robinson offers forest bathing in Los Angeles:

In LA, we mostly take the city sounds around us for granted. We tune them out with our own talking or driving or whatever media we are listening to or watching, and we make some amazing and wonderful sounds here, in music, television, movies, festivals, sports, and the thrum of everyday life in the city.

However, there is another soundscape out there, and when we get quiet and listen it's amazing what we discover.

In my work we always do sound meditations. We just stop talking, stop walking, get quiet, close our eyes for a few minutes, and notice what we hear. We are usually not deep in the woods, where we expect to hear sounds of nature. We might be in a city park, or garden, or a canyon trail in the Santa Monica Mountains. There's still possibly a lot of city or traffic sounds, but there is something else too, something that we can only discover when we get quiet.

It's a really simple practice, but people are usually astounded that in a big, noisy city they can hear so many birds singing, and they can hear coyotes howling at night. If they listen a little longer and embrace that stillness, they can hear more. They hear a particular bird, like a red-winged blackbird, and that stirs a memory for them. They may suddenly hear, or notice, the sounds of wind in the trees or waves crashing on the beach if they are near the ocean. These sounds are always there but we just aren't always listening, or we are busy making our own sounds.

Where I live, I hear traffic from the 90, from Lincoln Boulevard, but I also hear at certain times of day the high-pitched call of an osprey that soars above Ballona Creek. I love to hear that sound.

I do the sound meditation with grade school kids when they visit the Ballona Wetlands. They can hear lizards rustling through reed grass, bird songs, and even the sound of a duck's wings as it lands on water. It's thrilling the first time you hear that sound. The kids are surprised and excited.

We realize in these quiet but surprising moments how much is all around us, how we are immersed and in relationship with nature, even though we don't always see that, and we might not think about it very much.

In these moments of awe in the simple practice of listening, it can awaken something. It can help us remember, and hopefully appreciate, the reciprocity inherent in our relationship with nature; the enormous debt of gratitude we owe to the natural world for our very existence and our ongoing duty to be good caretakers of the earth.

Some research has found that meaningful experiences in nature at a young age are correlated with positive environmental behavior later in life. So, I think about that whenever I am at Ballona Wetlands with those first graders, listening for birds singing and lizards rustling through the grasses.

**Jill Robinson**
**Mindful Nature Guides**
**www.jrobholistichealth.com**

**Counsellor, Ecotherapist and Nature & Forest Therapy Guide, Estelle Asselin offers forest bathing in London:**
When you guide a forest bathing walk in a big city like London, you will have to deal with man-made noises during the session. I think the key to not make it an issue is first to acknowledge those sounds, not pretend they don't exist. It's about gently inviting people to notice them without focusing too much on them. Just like the rest of nature is actually doing.

Of course, people often comment on how it makes them realise how loud human beings are. And while it might not be a completely pleasant noticing, I believe it can be a helpful one in the long term, to change behaviours.

But people comment often also in a positive manner about these sounds.

I remember a woman saying she loved hearing people around us greeting each other and enjoying themselves. And a man, one day, described all the sounds that we could hear around us as a forest orchestra, with the planes being the double bass!

I believe as well that the practice of forest bathing supports people entering a different space, where they are totally immersed in nature and forget completely about time and ignore people passing by them and sounds that could appear disturbing.

Finally, I like guiding in the city because I'm committed to challenge the idea that there is "a good nature" and "a bad nature," a first-class and a second-class natural environment. And I believe that being connected to our local natural environment, and therefore to all its sounds, is much more valuable for people's well-being than only spending a week in a so-called wild place, for example.

Estelle Asselin
**THE CONNECTIVE SPACE**
**www.estelleasselin.com**

**Licensed Clinical Social Worker & Certified Nature & Forest Therapy Guide, Alyse Rynor offers forest bathing in Evanston, Illinois:**
I was just thinking about it the other day, as I walked with a small group along a natural area on McCormick Blvd. in Evanston. I realized that the cars were whizzing by, and it was as if I didn't even hear them. But I would say this about urban forest bathing (and I do take people into forest preserve areas, so it is more quiet...except for airplanes from O'Hare flying overhead), that isn't a disturbance.

It's as if spending time among the trees in urban areas causes something magical to happen. It's like the trees, bushes, plants, fields and flowers bring us into their world, blocking out the sounds of automobiles or even airplanes overhead. Recently, while guiding a small group, spending time engaging with trees and taking in the beautiful fall colors as we walked along the banks of a canal, cars were whizzing by only 25 yards away. Yet not one of us noticed the noise of the city, let alone were distracted by it. It was as if we had entered another time and place—one filled with nature, peace and the presence of connection.

**Alyse Rynor**
**Soul Choice Counseling**
**https://alyserynor.com**

**Certified Forest Bathing Guide, Al Estock offers forest bathing in Sweet Home Chicago:**
For me, forest bathing is about awareness, and a welcoming spirit of curiosity. Silence is a friend. Humans are part of nature...as are human sounds. How we receive what we hear is an individual process. Many humans have hearing challenges, and I am grateful for my changing abilities to hear. Again, for me, all sounds encountered are welcome... even if some may be momentarily distracting or annoying...and I may choose to alter my focus however I wish. Labeling sounds as noise is truly a personal judgment...and I do my best to try to let noise judgments go...sometimes easier said than done. My forest bathing experience is enhanced when I relax, and when I let whatever sounds I encounter flow through me... savoring any as I may choose, and letting the others gently go.

**Al Estock**
**aaestock@frontier.com**

**Certified Forest Bathing Guide, Carola Amtmann offers forest bathing in Mexico City:**

Here in Mexico City, I often guide forest bathing in a popular National Park called Desierto de los Leones nearby my home.

But other times, I've been at the Centro Historico (the historic center of Mexico City) between two of the most concurrent avenues doing a forest therapy walk with AMAZING results.

Even in the loudest city, in the busiest city, you can always find through your ears a bird singing, through your eyes leaves moving, though your fingers cortex of trees, and through your heart people surrounding you sometimes sharing your silence but sometimes looking at you saying like: "Oh I need time to stop like that girl is doing, right now."

Another thing that I already learned to do is to tell my groups that in life, especially life in Mexico City, we will always be around noise, some of them we like and some of them we don't...but let's take them as they are, as they come, without judging them, and that's a whole different and new experience.

Carola Amtmann
https://www.instagram.com/bosqueadentro/?hl=es

**Certified Forest Bathing Guide, Amanda Yik offers forest bathing in Hong Kong:**

Personally, I don't use the word "noise" during forest therapy walks because for most people, as the word suggests unpleasantness and disturbances, easily takes us to a place of judgment. I remember years ago, as a very new forest therapy guide, I guided a walk at one of my favourite places, and on that particular day, it was more crowded than I had ever seen before. The man-made sounds were relentless—music on loudspeakers; people talking, laughing, singing, dancing; children running around shouting and screaming; and these are on top of the usual distant traffic and the occasional aircraft flying above our heads.

When we paused for a round of sharing, one participant shared that she felt discouraged as she hadn't expected this place to be so noisy. When I heard that I had to admit I was disappointed too. However, another participant shared how she didn't mind at all, and in fact actually she enjoyed listening to all the sounds of people enjoying being outside on a beautiful day. I felt so deeply touched that I actually had tears running down my face. I couldn't help but reflect on these questions—What makes pleasant music, and what constitutes noise? Who gets to decide? What preconceptions am I holding when I listen to the sounds of a place? Who am I to say what is noise and what is not?

My preferred choice of word is therefore always "sounds," which simply refers to vibrations that travel through the air, because ultimately, that's what they are!

Amanda Yik
**Certified Nature and Forest Therapy Guide & Trainer**
**Certified Professional Coach for Transformation**
**www.shinrinyokuhk.com**

## Evening Guiding

An edge I experience is guiding at night. I enjoyed a recent invitation from the Michigan Department of Natural Resources to guide a forest bathing outing at the historic Ralph A. McMullen (RAM) Center in Roscommon. The RAM Center is a popular conference center on the shores of Higgins Lake with a dominant white cedar forest type. Since it is a rural area, without light pollution, it grows very dark there during twilight hours.

The first edge I felt was the responsibility of group safety. The fear of my guests tripping and falling or injuring themselves from low-hanging branches was intense. To prepare, I purchased twenty inexpensive, lightweight mini flashlights for the participants and handed them out when we began. I brought along solar landscaping lights and decorative strings of battery-powered mini lights. I scouted the area ahead of time to ensure trip hazards such as logs, roots, and rocks were avoided.

Through preparation, sharing awareness, and a little bit of luck, we made it through without bloody scratches or broken bones. The atmosphere is different at night and the participants didn't seem bothered by the darkness. In fact, I believe this evening guide stirred our primordial instincts and provoked excitement from wandering in the evening woods.

## Winter Guiding

Winter programming will bring out the bruisers. Anyone who engages in outdoor activities in areas where seasonal harsh weather conditions prevail will appreciate forest bathing in winter. Helpful reminders over proper footwear and layering, scouting for hazards, keeping invitations a bit shorter than you would in summer, providing warm tea and snacks, and possibly a campfire—where and when it is safe, legal, and appropriate—are good steps to take. Contact the land manager or owner to learn and follow the rules and regulations to have a campfire.

Winter brings on a peaceful serenity for wandering. It is nature's time for rest and that can be felt along a snowy forest trail. Try guiding in winter at least once to experience the differences in seasons and participant response.

## Guiding Kids

As Tilden reminded us, interpretive programs for children should not just be watered down versions of adult programs, but custom-designed considering age-appropriateness. The same rules apply for forest bathing across the generations. For three decades I've used multi-sensory nature exploration activities and programs for children, yet I'll admit, guiding forest bathing for kids is edgy for me and I'm sure it boils down to a matter of putting to practice the thought of letting go of trying to control outcomes with the exciting level of unpredictability that kids typically provide.

But kids are so engaged and honest with their journeyings and sharing. They never fail to fully immerse themselves in the experience. Forest bathing with young ones promotes and instills solutions to stress, problem solving, and healthy habits that may last a lifetime. An added layer of safety for children could include establishing and pointing out clear and obvious "wandering boundaries" for young participants to stay within using flagging or cones and recruiting the assistance of adults to move along quietly with the kids to ensure no one gets lost. To ensure good communication when preparing a forest bathing program is to consider your target audience. Confusion or disappointment can be avoided by indicating whether your program is geared toward adults only, family-friendly (kids and adults), or for kids only during the planning and registration process.

## They're Just Not That into You: Ecoincluding the Selectively Inclusive

Science reveals how the healing effects of forest bathing are universally beneficial, but not everyone is down with this practice. Sometimes it's as hard to find support within our communities as it is to offer. As a guide, you'll encounter folks who won't even disguise their bias. I tried to encourage a colleague to join me for a forest bathing program and they responded, "Yeah, yeah! Then we can share survival strategies in the woods, and—" I interrupted them, "That's not how this works. Forest bathing is not about roughing it in the wilderness, it's about exploring how the trees make you feel."

"HOW THE TREES MAKE YOU FEEL?" They were out.

For people who refuse to try the practice of forest bathing or those along for the ride who were dragged to a program by friends, the concepts are edgy. Too tree-huggy, too hippie, too weird. Some might draw their own conclusions that they'll be asked to do something silly or embarrassing. In actuality, the practice is a mostly personal, quiet, somber experience. Certainly, guides do welcome anything that arrives, but forest bathing is a restorative sensory exploration combining rest and wandering, interspersed with facilitated group gatherings and solo time. The emphasis is on unplugging, slowing down, and awakening the senses without having to "do" anything.

Yet for some, their edginess about the unknown of trying something new makes it entirely possible that some might bounce before your program ends or decide that it was not for them before you even get started. Fellow guides have shared stories of people who spazzed out in a complete meltdown in front of the group before storming off. I had a participant say aloud, "Is this when we drink the Kool-Aid?" during a lovely tea ceremony I laid out during one program's conclusion. *Oh my God, what?*

It's sometimes challenging to fully embrace skeptics when they identify themselves, but modeling ease, providing choice, and employing other concepts of trauma-informed care is the best way to let it roll. Like interpretive programs, every forest bathing outing will have its own unique energy and balance. Welcome whatever arrives.

When planning forest bathing for visitors, start anywhere. If you are an interpretive supervisor who somehow does not personally develop and lead interpretive programs you might consider hiring a professional forest bathing guide for your sites: www.forestbathingfinder.com, www.natureandforesttherapy.earth/guides. (*Pro tip*: Interpretive leaders really should nix their programming obsolescence. Because leadership?) If you are an interpreter who wants to try guiding, the sample outlined in Chapter 5 is available for you to use and adapt. If you're like me, you prefer to learn by example from a professional guide (find someone local from the links above). Meanwhile, why not go ahead and plan that winter forest bathing program for your visitors? Don't make room for analysis paralysis. You've got this.

## Case Study: Sensory Explorations with Touch-Me-Nots?

So, when is a jewelweed more than a jewelweed? When it helps illustrate an interpretive theme and encourages visitors to use their senses during an interpretive discovery experience.

Using multi-sensory experiences for presenting one stop on an interpretive hike, it's important to look at the planning for the total interpretive hike of which the jewelweed trail stop is but one example.

The interpretive theme was: *"Nature has created a variety of unique ways for plants to disperse their seeds. On today's walk you'll discover and experience several of them in surprising ways."*

Then every interpretive program should be based on interpretive objectives.

Upon completion of the interpretive hike the majority of visitors will have experienced:

- Learning Objectives (all visitors will be able to name at least 3 unique ways plants have evolved to disperse their seeds).
- Behavioral Objectives (all visitors will be able to use several of their 5 senses to experience and discover how plants disperse their seeds).
- Emotional Objectives (the majority of visitors will be surprised at the creative ways plants disperse their seeds and be curious to learn more about them).

So, in preparing for the interpretive program, we should have our theme that all stops on the hike will illustrate, and know what objectives need to be addressed to develop each individual hike stop interpretation.

Jewelweed was one of my favorite plants to interpret to visitors when I was leading interpretive hikes as a seasonal naturalist with Ohio State Parks back in my youth.

At this stop some real surprises. The story of jewelweed, also known as "touch-me-not," arises from its long history and scientifically proven efficacy in treating all sorts of skin irritations, including poison ivy. It's especially valuable for anglers and anyone who regularly visits stream banks and moist woodland paths where stinging nettles are found. Should you brush your leg or hands/arms against the nettles (ouch!), crush up some of the jewelweed plant stems—they're very moist—and rub the juice on the itchy area. Let's give it a try as an example. It does work to stop the itching. I also brought some jewelweed spray with me for you to try as well if you have an itch. Now this is real, as I've done it and used it (spraying some of the jewelweed spray on visitors itch if they want to try it).

But this plant has another surprise. When the flower produces a small green bean looking seed pod (you can see them on these plants if you look closely), the pod is spring loaded to "shoot" robin's-egg blue seeds out from the plant—quite a surprise. Let's give it a try. I'll put some "armed" pods in your hand and then I'll count to three and then we can touch the pods in your hand, and we'll see what happens. WOW! Thus, the name "touch-me-not."

Bang! Seeds are shot out from the pod, and then you can peel off the dark seed coat and expose the robin's-egg blue seeds like this (demonstration for visitors to try).

By the way here's another discovery. The little blue seeds taste like almonds. So go ahead and give them a taste.

Now you've seen and tasted the rest of the "touch-me-not" story I've been itching to tell you about and you experienced another way plants can disperse their seeds.

So that's one case study example in incorporating sensory experiences into interpretive programs. But there's another reason:

Visitors remember:

- 10% of what they hear;
- 20% of what they read;

- 50% of what they see;
- And 90% of what they do!

So, using multiple senses in interpretive programs (active participation) enhances memory retention of the hike's interpretive experiences and the interpretive theme of the program.

And that's the real "rest of the story."

Prof John A. Veverka | Director, The Heritage Interpretation Training Center
Interpretive archaeologist, World Heritage planner, professor and author

"*Everything is hard before it is easy.*"
—Goethe

# Chapter 5

## THE TREES AWAIT US

A friend cautioned against oversharing when learning of this chapter. They worried I'd shortchange myself by giving away too many trade secrets, but I don't believe in carrying program ideas close to the vest. I never understood that approach. As a certified forest therapy guide and a park interpreter of advancing years it's in my bloodstream to provoke connections between people and the land. I've always shared styles, strategies, activities, and ideas from my programs along the way to enlist others into adopting a stewardship mindset. Because when you come right down to it, there is room in the pool for everyone. Why else are we here?

Continued practice and trust in the process, trust in your audience, and trust in yourself as a guide lays the foundation for growth and meaningful experiences when forest bathing with groups. Start small. Practice by yourself and then move on to guiding little groups of family or close friends if it helps build confidence to ease into guiding for public audiences. Some might prefer to practice guiding people they do not know over those they do. Whatever feels right to you is the way you begin. This chapter offers a planning schedule and sample program plan as a springboard into guiding.

**A word on this outline:**
You don't have to use the entire outline. You can opt to pull parts from it and weave them into your existing interpretive programs. Or use this

framework for one or two forest bathing programs, and afterwards begin adjusting the style, invitations, or approach and reinvent a plan that works for you, your site, and your visitors.

The invitations described in this chapter are merely suggestions to get your feet wet. Experienced guides grow to use what the land is offering the day of the program. Windy day = wind invitation: "Meander and notice how the breeze feels on your skin," cloudy day = cloud invitation: "Sit and notice the shapes of the clouds," evening program = evening invitation: "Close your eyes and listen for the last bird you heard."

Make certain that you personally participate in all the invitations that you offer the group. It demonstrates your embrace of and commitment to the practice.

**A word on props/supplies/materials:**
Keep in mind that any suggested "props" used in the outline below, such as musical instruments, paper, writing utensils, etc., *are not required* to successfully implement forest bathing outings. This is a practice that doesn't have to cost much money to implement. The only truly necessary supplies needed during a program are tea, cups, and a teapot or thermos for tea ceremony, all of which could be purchased at a second-hand store. When guiding blind audiences, it may be helpful to have an instrument to let guests know when to return from an invitation. When guiding deaf participants, it may be helpful to bring colored flagging or flashing lights, or setting cell phones to vibrate to receive a text or alarm letting the guests know when to return from an invitation and using chalkboards or braille scrolls to communicate invitations and receive shares.

I often prepare scrolls with prompts (examples at the end of Chapter 2) when offering certain invitations, such as "Find Your Spot." Any perceived needs for guiding forest bathing can be improvised through the creative freedom of the guide using varied invitations. Whether the guide wants to keep the program basic, or take it next level, a list of resources is provided following the Appendix.

**A word about catching and crafting invitations:**
New forest bathing guides should learn a few invitations to replicate during their first programs, but as guides develop their own unique style, the goal is to fully work in partnership with the land, abandoning memorized plans and instinctively catching invitations based on what the land is offering. If there is surface water nearby, craft a water invitation such as, *"Find a sit spot near the pond and notice tiny life in the water."* If there is a breeze blowing through the forest during your program, craft a wind invitation such as, *"Wander slowly and notice how the breeze feels on your face."*

The language of invitation gently prompts people to sensory connections using simple, open, sensory, and infinite invitations. Invitation is not evocation. Invitations are not exercises, activities, or assignments. Invitations can be lengthy or short, but all involve connecting the senses with the more-than-human world. Remind your participants that there are no expectations or wrong ways to do the invitations.

The idea is to get people out of their heads and back to a focus on the body and sensory explorations in nature. It can be edgy, but it takes trust in the forest, trust in the participants, trust in the process, and trust in ourselves.

If you happen to be using a narrow trail, suggest participants move in a different direction for each invitation for a change of scenery—unless they really enjoy going to the same spot that originally called to them.

**A word on your guiding practice growth:**
Get certified! Demonstrating the commitment of a certification is principal in building confidence with yourself and with your audience. Several organizations including ANFT offer incredible online cohorts and in-person immersions in various time zones throughout the year to round off your professional portfolio. The organization also offers outstanding year-round online and in-person workshops for continued development. Contact information on ANFT and resources are found in the Appendix.

## Profile of Mood States

Profile of Mood States, also known as POMS, are questionnaires or surveys first created in 1971 by Douglas M. McNair, Maurie Lorr, and Leo F. Droppleman. The original purpose of POMS was to serve as a baseline or a building block to gauge psychological moods of patients from across a spectrum of mental and physical illnesses and diseases. Its use plays an important role in stress management and pain management, helping athletes, senior citizens, and other demographics.

The original form consisted of sixty-four questions but was shortened through revisions by other researchers down to thirty-four questions. Now there are many versions of the survey and you can create your own version. This example below is a short-form (POMS-SF) version created by psychologists Curran, Andrykowski, and Studts in 1995. Distributing POMS helps forest bathing audiences gauge their emotions before and after forest bathing. The intent is not to share with the guide, or share with the other participants, it is a personal assessment of how the impact of forest bathing lands within them.

Consider customizing a POMS questionnaire for your forest bathing programs.

POMS-SF (reprinted with permission)

**Below is a list of words that describe feelings people have. Please read each one carefully. Then circle ONE answer to the right which best describes HOW YOU HAVE BEEN FEELING DURING THE <u>PAST WEEK</u> INCLUDING TODAY.**

**The numbers refer to these phrases:**
**0 = Not at all**
**1 = A little**
**3 = Moderately**
**3 = Quite a bit**
**4 = Extremely**

| 1. | Tense | 0 1 2 3 4 |
|---|---|---|
| 2. | Angry | 0 1 2 3 4 |
| 3. | Worn Out | 0 1 2 3 4 |
| 4. | Unhappy | 0 1 2 3 4 |
| 5. | Lively | 0 1 2 3 4 |
| 6. | Confused | 0 1 2 3 4 |
| 7. | Peeved | 0 1 2 3 4 |
| 8. | Sad | 0 1 2 3 4 |
| 9. | Active | 0 1 2 3 4 |
| 10. | On Edge | 0 1 2 3 4 |
| 11. | Grouchy | 0 1 2 3 4 |
| 12. | Blue | 0 1 2 3 4 |
| 13. | Energetic | 0 1 2 3 4 |
| 14. | Hopeless | 0 1 2 3 4 |
| 15. | Uneasy | 0 1 2 3 4 |
| 16. | Restless | 0 1 2 3 4 |
| 17. | Unable to Concentrate | 0 1 2 3 4 |
| 18. | Fatigued | 0 1 2 3 4 |
| 19. | Annoyed | 0 1 2 3 4 |
| 20. | Discouraged | 0 1 2 3 4 |
| 21. | Resentful | 0 1 2 3 4 |
| 22. | Nervous | 0 1 2 3 4 |
| 23. | Miserable | 0 1 2 3 4 |
| 24. | Cheerful | 0 1 2 3 4 |
| 25. | Bitter | 0 1 2 3 4 |
| 26. | Exhausted | 0 1 2 3 4 |
| 27. | Anxious | 0 1 2 3 4 |
| 28. | Helpless | 0 1 2 3 4 |
| 29. | Weary | 0 1 2 3 4 |
| 30. | Bewildered | 0 1 2 3 4 |
| 31. | Furious | 0 1 2 3 4 |
| 32. | Full of Pep | 0 1 2 3 4 |
| 33. | Worthless | 0 1 2 3 4 |
| 34. | Forgetful | 0 1 2 3 4 |
| 35. | Vigorous | 0 1 2 3 4 |
| 36. | Uncertain about Things | 0 1 2 3 4 |
| 37. | Bushed | 0 1 2 3 4 |

## Sample forest bathing plan:

**Hospitality** is a familiar tradition for park interpreters. It often takes place at the trailhead parking lot with a greeting, personal welcome, and housekeeping for participants. It is the opportunity to share helpful announcements such as if/where there are bathrooms, cell phone courtesies, and other information such as when the program will conclude. Because you are holding time for others as a guide, it is important to honor the time of your participants. This means it's OK to start just a few minutes late if you are waiting for people, but make sure to conclude the program when you promised it would conclude and share that, "In order to honor everyone's time today, we will be concluding by or before this time frame____."

Invite participants to communicate if any needs arise during the program. The purpose of Hospitality is to emulate warm accompaniment for participants. Ask the group to take a double-sided POM survey at this point to gauge any changes in mood from now until the program's conclusion. Tell them the survey is not for you nor is it to share (unless they'd like to after the program). It is only for them. Remind them to take the second survey on the backside of the page in their car after the program and notice any differences in mood from start to finish.

Move the group from the parking area to a pre-selected place at the start of your forest trail. Take a moment to share **Awareness** for the group. This could mean mentioning the existence of poison ivy, or other risks such as tree roots, slippery rocks, ticks, snakes, and larger wildlife. You can also mention the possibility of encountering other people along the trail who are not with your group. The idea is not to conjure unease but establish trust through sharing awareness of the surroundings. Invite participants to share any needs that you might accommodate. These steps help communicate, "I've got you covered."

Move onto **Introductions**. Begin by acknowledging the original wildland tenders (see my descriptions in the first paragraph of Chapter 3). Share the path of the watershed. Then move along the circle, starting with whoever would like to go first, introducing each other. To keep track of timing, ask for their name, where they traveled from to be here today, and what is their favorite tree. You can opt to use a stone, a pinecone, or some object that they can use to pass to one another as each introduction is made.

Since many people have never experienced forest bathing, they often arrive at the program with questions about its origins and nomenclature. Among professional guides, the jury is still out on this, because some view oversharing or talking too much at participants may shape their experience or outcomes and the idea is to allow people the freedom to interpret and engage in the immersion however they wish. I'm in the camp that feels it is completely appropriate and often appreciated when guides begin by providing some historical context first, before jumping right in. Consider adapting the history outlined in Chapter 1 followed by this narrative:

*A guide is not there to speak for the forest. A guide is there to create space for the forest to speak. The forest is the therapist, a guide opens doors and holds time and space for mindfulness in nature and forging authentic relationships with nature. I guide therapeutic explorations with accompaniment. Forest therapy is the prefect reminder to "be here now."*

*I work in partnership with the more-than-human world to accompany and support others on the journeys through which they encounter and embody the whole of who they are. I'll offer several sensory invitations that you can choose to participate in or not. And there is no wrong way to do any of the invitations. How you do them, if you choose to, will be the right way.*

*There are no expected outcomes of today's program. Spending time outdoors for just a short period of time is an opportunity to get out of our heads and back into our bodies. And that can be an edgy idea to some, to be reminded to be inside our bodies. It takes trust to welcome whatever comes. For today's outing we will hold a safe space for each other and welcome choice and witnessing and kindness and reciprocity.*

*We begin with a land acknowledgment of the First Nations; the traditional and current wild tenders of this land we are occupying. Acknowledge the watershed or bioregion.*

*I'd like to take this opportunity to have you each introduce yourselves to the group. We will pass around this pinecone and when it is passed to you, please share your name, where you're from and what is your favorite tree?*

After introductions, move the group down the trail and stop at a pre-determined spot that has space for the group size.

## Arrival

*This is our opportunity to "shake off the road dust" and fully arrive in this forest. You can choose to sit or stand here as we arrive at this place. It's not necessary to face the circle—feel comfortable to spread out and face any direction staying within range of my voice.*

*Gently shift your weight left and right. You might slowly roll your head or your shoulders. Take this moment to check in with your body and see if anything needs adjusting and nest into your spot.*

Recite each sensory exploration below with slow pauses in between the short invitations.

*Look around to the left side of your body moving your gaze slowly from up in the tree canopy to eye-level then down on the ground. Become aware of what is on your left. Next, look to your right and do the same: gaze up in the canopy first, check out what is up overhead, then slowly to eye-level and then down on the ground noticing everything on the right side of your body. You might turn to look behind you on either side of your body. Keep in mind that as we see or experience this place, the forest is also aware of us, acknowledges that we are here, and welcomes us. The wildlife hear us, smell us, and some can certainly see us, and the trees and other plants are taking in our carbon dioxide.*

I invite you now to close your eyes—or if you prefer not to close your eyes—soften your gaze to rest and relax your eye muscles after a long week of screen time.

Spend time feeling the wind on our face.

Notice how it feels on our cheeks and chin, or any exposed parts of our neck and chest.

Focus on breathing naturally for a few moments. I invite you to take a few quiet, slow inhales and soft, steady exhales through your nose with your mouth closed. Notice any smells the wind or the air is carrying and what that smell might be, where it's coming from.

Try inhaling again deeply and slowly a few times using your mouth to inhale as if gently sucking air through a straw. Notice any tastes in the wind or the air. Perhaps it might be the last thing you ate that you are still tasting. Reflect on what it's like to have a sense of taste.

What are the sounds you are hearing in the wind? Which are furthest away, which are closest?

Notice how the smells, tastes, or sounds in the wind land with you, in your body.

Bring to mind the journey of wind. Where it traveled before it arrived here, where it's going?

Put your hand on your chest and feel the rise and fall of your natural breathing. Notice how your breathing is a part of the symphony of this place.

*Consider sharing a private thought or even a sound with the wind however you would like.*

*Slowly begin to open your eyes or refocus your gaze and return your attention to the group. Your presence here is enough but if anyone would like to share one word describing how that landed with you. If you don't care to share you don't have to, simply pass to the next person. Who would like to go first?*

Wait patiently—it may take what seems like a long span of uncomfortable silence until someone finally speaks up to share, but someone will break the silence. Make sure everyone gets a chance to share or to pass by going around in a circle, to the right or left of the first person to share. As the guide you should share too but avoid being the first person to speak at the conclusion of the invitations.

## Slow Your Roll

*Moving slowly is challenging for some. Often our mind begins to race through cycles of distraction, but after a while, our focus shifts to the present and we can find an inner calmness. I invite you all to give each other space to wander "alone together" and notice: What's in motion? What is moving around you? What makes it move? We will engage in this invitation in silence, and I will lead our group as we slowly stroll down the trail.*

*Please be aware of your footing and low hanging branches or any obstacles in your path. Move about slowly.*

Lead the group slowly and silently or using a musical instrument such as an earth flute or pan drum. Once arriving at next location:

*Your presence here is enough but I welcome anyone to share how slowing down landed in your body. What are you noticing? And if you care to share, start with the prompt, "I am noticing." When you are finished sharing, motion to pass to the person next to you. If you don't care to share, pass to the person next to you. Who would like to go first?*

Make sure everyone gets a chance to share or pass by going around in a circle, to the right or left of the first person to share.

## FIRST PARTNER INVITATION

### Find Your Spot

*To begin, I invite you to find a stick from two to four feet long. When you find one, place the stick on the ground in front of your feet, making sure the ends are touching the ends of other sticks next to it to form a full circle.*

Once all sticks are arranged in a circle on the ground in front of the group, place the container of scrolls in the center of the group circle. Then share what happens next:

*I invite you to step into the circle one at a time, crossing over this threshold and select one scroll. Take the scroll with you to a spot that calls to you. Once you find your spot, get comfortable in your space whether you choose to sit or stand. Then open and read your scroll.*

*I'll call everyone back to this circle where we are now with the pan drum, it will sound like this (tap a few times on the drum) in thirty minutes. When you return, make sure you cross back into the circle first, then step out of the circle as an indicator that you are fully back with us. I'll keep track of time, so you don't have to. Please be aware of your footing and low hanging branches or any obstacles in your path. Move about slowly.*

After thirty minutes, use the pan drum to call the group back. As each participant crosses back into the circle and out again, welcome them back one at a time by name.

Once the group is back:

*Your presence here is enough but I welcome anyone to share how that invitation landed with you, in your body. What are you noticing? Begin your answer with, "I am noticing." When you are finished sharing, motion*

Forest bathing with visitors at Oden State Fish Hatchery, Oden, Michigan. *Photo by Mo Stine.*

*to pass to the person next to you. If you don't care to share, pass to the person next to you.*

Wait patiently until someone speaks up and make sure everyone gets a chance to share or pass by going around in a circle, to the right or left of the first person to share.

## SECOND PARTNER INVITATION (have any type of paper and writing utensil available for each participant)

### WHO ELSE IS HERE?

Distribute paper and something to write with to everyone.

*Giving each other space, I invite you to wander slowly and notice a being of the more-than-human world. Let whatever it is emerge naturally to your gaze like a slow reveal. Is the being moving? Is it static? How did it come to arrive here? Perhaps you might draw a sketch of the being or write something down about noticing them. Perhaps you will head in a different direction along the trail for a change of scenery from your first invitation.*

*I'll call everyone back to the circle where we are now with these chimes (sound chimes) in twenty minutes. I'll keep track of time, so you don't have to. Some things to be aware of are low hanging branches or objects that you might trip over.*

After twenty minutes, sound chimes. Once group returns:

*Your presence here is enough but I welcome anyone to share how that invitation landed with you, in your body. What are you noticing? And if you care to share, start by saying, "I am noticing." When you are finished sharing, motion to pass to the person next to you.*

Wait patiently until someone speaks up and make sure everyone gets a chance to share or pass by going around in a circle, to the right or left of the first person to share.

## FINAL PARTNER INVITATION

### A HANDFUL OF FOREST

*Meander on the trail and seek out an object. Anything that calls your attention to it. After you find the object, stay where you are and take the object into your hands and feel its surface with your fingertips. Is it rough? Smooth? Squishy? Is it cold or warm? How did this object form? How did it come to be here? Perhaps you can tell a secret to the object that no one else knows.*

*Bring your object back with you to share when I'll call everyone back to this place where we are now with the coyote call—it will sound like this, and this time I want you all to answer me back in a loud coyote call. Let's practice (guide gives coyote call, group responds with coyote call). We will do this invitation for ten minutes. I'll keep track of time. Please be aware of your footing and low hanging branches or any obstacles in your path. Move about slowly. Perhaps you will move in another completely different direction along the trail for a change of scenery from your first and second invitations.*

After ten minutes, give the coyote call—group responds. Once group arrives back:

*I invite you to bring your object to the tea table one at a time, and one at a time, discuss why you selected the object. When you are done, place your object on our tea table and motion to the person next to you. When everyone is done sharing, we will create an artistic totem together by placing objects on the ground in whatever pattern we create.*

Set up for tea ceremony after the group sets out to gather. Spread out cloth or blanket, arrange teacups, and pot, snacks, and any natural items you wish to use to decorate the setting. It is often not necessary to use a table—the ground can be the table—but consider the physical ability of your participants to bend down or reach items.

## TEA CEREMONY

Announce that tea ceremony is a means to return from liminality to the tamed world that awaits us, and this final time together helps us return to our minds. Pour the first cup of tea for the land, to thank the forest for providing us shelter, oxygen, and its beauty. Remind participants that they do not have to drink the tea if they don't care to but at least accept tea and perhaps pour theirs out onto the land in a similar fashion as a gesture of thanks to the forest. Hand a cup of tea to each participant thanking each of them by name for coming. Inform participants that the tea you have brewed includes eastern white pine needles so that they will take the forest with them when drinking it in. Invite participants to enjoy a snack.

During tea: For this final gathering, read a short poem or short essay to close.

After reading, ask everyone:
*Is there anything you'd like to share to make the program complete?*
Make sure everyone gets a chance to share or pass.

*This completes our program.*
Pack up while remaining available to those who stick around to share stories or ask questions on your way back to the parking lot.

Remind participants to complete the second side of their POM survey in their cars to assess any noticeable changes in mood.

---

## Case Study: Wild Ride Night Bike

Kejimkujik National Park and National Historic site, situated in the middle of the Southwest Nova Scotia Biosphere Reserve, is not the type of place that you drive through and quickly stop and take pictures of colossal, majestic views, and hop back in your car and keep going. It is much, much deeper than that, and is a place that requires you to slow down, zoom in, and get yourself out into to really experience its essence. Parks Canada interpreters know just how to guide you to the magic, with carefully crafted immersive and experiential programs to help visitors connect to nature and Mi'kmaq culture, to themselves, and to each other.

Kejimkujik Interpreters have recently embarked on the creation of some more experiential and embodied forms of interpretation, using people's five (and more?) senses as an entry point to present-centered, mindfulness/mind-shifting programming. Being a

---

dark-sky reserve (since 2010), interpreters have made use of complete darkness in the forests and on the waterways, and even on roadways, to heighten the visitors' other senses.

One sensory-based program that is having a very profound effect on visitors is the Wild Ride Night Bike. Two interpreters, one who is Indigenous (Mi'kmaq), guide up to 12 visitors on their bicycles on the paved Main Parkway. There is one catch: the program takes place in the total darkness with only red lights to guide their way! This 2.5-hour program takes visitors out of their regular sense-perception worlds and brings them into a nocturnal landscape allowing time for their vision to adjust to what seems like pure darkness. During the bike ride, there are really only two stops.

One stop, beside an endangered turtle's protected habitat, is where visitors are asked to get in touch with their other instincts and senses, now that their sense of sight is very inhibited. They are told about the baby Blanding's Turtle, who emerges from its egg with all the instincts/senses it needs to survive. Visitors are asked to get in touch with their other senses, including their back body and their peripheral vision. They are also taught the Mi'kmaq perspective of colour, which is focused on "becoming" a colour and "not becoming" a colour, depending on the amount of light shining on it.

The second stop is a blind taste test! The visitors are asked to reach out in front of them where there is a paper bag that contains five items. The items are meant to tune in to the five types of taste: umami, sweet, sour, bitter, and salty. The visitors open their bag and start to nibble away at the five different individually packaged items, and they have to figure out which is which. The visitors are blown away by how their taste buds are heightened and how the taste test in the dark gives them a different perspective on eating foods and eating them more mindfully.

After the blind taste test is done the visitors get back on their bicycles and pedal all the way back to the beginning of the hike and, on the way, the lead interpreter turns on a very loud speaker that is blasting, dark-sky themed pop music such as "Rocket Man" and "Midnight Train to Georgia." So as visitors are biking back to the beginning, they are following the sound of inspiring music and experiencing what feels like a whole different realm of the park in the darkness, with some red lights to guide them.

By the end of the Night Bike, it is as if the visitors have gone to another planet and come back. Their senses are more heightened, and they are more embodied, and in the moment. When visitors are forced to not rely on their sense of sight in the Dark Sky Preserve, their perspective completely shifts and they get much more in touch with their other senses, especially when an interpreter is there to guide them through a truly transformative sensory experience.

The Trees Await Us

*Photo by Parks Canada/*
*Nicole Boutilier*

*Photo by Parks Canada/*
*Ashley Moffat*

**Ashley Moffat** (*Bow*) | **Coordonnateur d'interprétation III, Kejimkujik**
**National Park & National Historic Site of Canada, Nova Scotia, Canada**

*"There is something in the nature of tea that leads us into a world of quiet contemplation of life."*
—Lin Yutang

Chapter 6

—

# ANATOMY OF A TEA CEREMONY

As we conclude every forest bathing outing with tea ceremony, so shall I conclude this book. The history of human consumption of tea is a bit ambiguous, likely dating back thousands of years for medicine, enjoyment, and mindfulness, and researching its history was powerful. Its use began in China where the tea plant (*Camellia sinensis*) is native. Tea stans can find endless resources and books, articles, recipes, websites, and blogs about the beverage's rich and violent history of taxation, smuggling, colonization, and wars, or its vastly proven health benefits. Tea is an elixir of life.

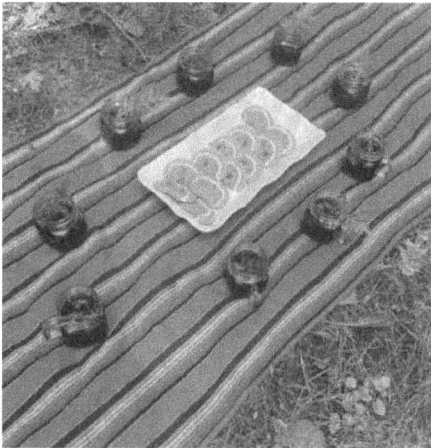

Watermelon cookies with summer tea service are typically a hit. Search ideas for recipes.

Consuming tea triggers nerve impulses in the brain to release hormones that produce a sense of calm. Drinking tea also keeps our mind clear, prompts rest, improves our attention span, helps us focus, and boosts antioxidants in our bloodstream, promoting health and wellness.

The tea ceremony closes our forest bathing excursions, and we refer to this part of the program as the **Threshold of Incorporation**, in which

Toasting with tea after winter forest bathing. (L-R) Ian, Heidi (background), Kerri, Jen. *Photo by Mo Stine.*

participants are offered a way out of the liminality of sensory explorations and prepare to re-enter the tamed world. This is the time for final gathering, sharing, and listening in order to make their time feel complete. The time to thank the forest for its reciprocity. For fresh oxygen, for safe spaces, for sharing its beauty with us.

Guides may choose to use tea purchased from the grocery store or make their own. When seeking plants to use in tea, keep in mind ethical harvesting. Basic guidelines include:

Winter forest bathing tea service.

1. Enter the forest with a plan, which includes knowing what exactly you are seeking, dressing appropriately for the weather and insect conditions, bringing water, gloves, proper pruning tools, and your cell phone or telling someone where you are headed and how long you will be gone, and knowing the legality and ethics of collecting on the land.
2. Be able to identify the species you are seeking with 100% accuracy. You could kill yourself or someone else by consuming poisonous plants. Take a tour with a professional botanist before heading out.
3. Ask permission of the plant before you cut.
4. Quietly await an answer.
5. Take only what you need from the forest and leave the area as good or better than you found it.

## Eastern White Pine Tea*

1. **Snip fresh needles from a tree and trim off any brown or dry parts**
2. **Rinse needles thoroughly in cold water**
3. **Trim needles to about one-inch pieces**
4. **Boil water in a pot and remove pot from heat once a rolling boil begins**
5. **Seep needles in the hot water for five to fifteen minutes depending on how strong you prefer your tea**
6. **Strain needles from the pot and pour water into a mug, adding lemon or honey**

To prepare for tea ceremony, share an invitation with your group, and while they are dispersed, lay out a blanket, tablecloth, or tapestry on any relatively flat ground available and decorate the area with iced tea glasses or hot teacups (based upon season or mood), non-allergenic snacks, and a few items from nature like stones, twigs, acorns, or cones. Call everyone back to gather around the tea service. Pour the first cup for the forest before sharing a cup with others. Remind participants that they do not have to drink the tea if they don't want to, but at least accept the tea and pour it out for the forest. Ask the group if anyone wants to share anything that will make their experience complete. Give everyone a chance to share or pass. During the final share, I always go last, after everyone else has shared their thoughts, and conclude each forest bathing tea ceremony with the words of Ralph Waldo Emerson:

*Finish each day and be done with it, you did what you could. Some absurdities and blunders no doubt crept in, forget them as soon as you can. Tomorrow is a new day. Begin it serenely and with too high a spirit to be encumbered by your old nonsense.*

*\*Consult a doctor about drinking pine tea if you are pregnant or nursing.*

# REFERENCES

## Chapter 1

Beck, L. & Cable, T. (2002). *Interpretation for the 21st Century: Fifteen Guiding Principles for Interpreting Nature and Culture, Second Edition.* Champaign, IL: Sagamore Publishing.

*Infographics - Screen Time Vs. Lean Time | DNPAO | CDC.* www.cdc.gov/nccdphp/dnpao/multimedia/infographics/getmoving.html. Accessed 5 July, 2022.

Kimmerer, R. (2013). *Braiding Sweetgrass: Indigenous Wisdom, Scientific Knowledge, and the Teachings of Plants.* Minneapolis, MN: Milkweed Editions.

*Last Child in the Woods* by Richard Louv, copyright © 2005. Reprinted by permission of Algonquin Books, an imprint of Hachette Book Group, Inc.

Li, Q. (2018). *Forest Bathing: How Trees Can Help You Find Health and Happiness.* New York, NY: Viking.

Mazzola, N., Willey, T. "Silver Birch Cohort." Association of Nature and Forest Therapy Guides and Programs, http://www.anft.earth.

Moore, Paul A. (2016). *The Hidden Power of Smell: How Chemicals Influence Our Lives and Behavior.* Bowling Green, OH: Springer.

Rideout, V., Foehr, U., Roberts, D. "Generation M2 Media in the Lives of 8- to 18-Year-Olds." Keiser Family Foundation, 2010. https://www.kff.org/wp-content/uploads/2013/01/8010.pdf. Accessed 25 August, 2022.

Tilden, F. (1957, 1968, 1977). *Interpreting Our Heritage, Third Edition.* Chapel Hill, NC: The University of North Carolina Press.

Wikipedia contributors. "History of science and technology in Japan." *Wikipedia, The Free Encyclopedia*. Wikipedia, The Free Encyclopedia, 5 Dec. 2022. Web. 20 Dec. 2022.

Wikipedia contributors. "Phytoncide." *Wikipedia, The Free Encyclopedia*. Wikipedia, The Free Encyclopedia, 6 Sep. 2022. Web. 20 Dec. 2022.

Wikipedia contributors. "Right to disconnect." *Wikipedia, The Free Encyclopedia*. Wikipedia, The Free Encyclopedia, 10 Jul. 2022. Web. 26 Dec. 2022.

Wohlleben, P. (2015). *The Hidden Life of Trees: What They Feel, How They Communicate*. Vancouver, CA: Graystone Books.

## Chapter 2

Defoe, Daniel. (1897). *Robinson Crusoe*. New York, Boston [etc.]: University publishing company.

Doherty, Meghan. (2013). *How Not to Be a Dick: An Everyday Etiquette Guide*. Minneapolis, MN: Zest Books.

Fitzwilliams-Heck, C. (2021). *A Practical Guide to Nature Study, Third Edition*. Dubuque, IA: Kendall Hunt Publishing Co.

Golding, William. (1954). *Lord of the Flies*. London, GB: Faber & Faber.

Hackenmiller, S. (2019). *The Outdoor Adventurer's Guide to Forest Bathing: Using Shinrin-Yoku to Hike, Bike, Paddle, and Climb Your Way to Health and Happiness*. Lanham, MD: Falcon Guides.

Haines, S. (2019). *The Politics of Trauma*. Berkeley, CA: North Atlantic Books.

Homer-Dixon, T. (2006). *The Upside of Down: Catastrophe, Creativity, and the Renewal of Civilization*. Toronto, CA: Vintage Canada.

"No FEAR Act." *FEMA.gov*, www.fema.gov/about/organization /equal-rights/no-fear-act. Accessed 10 October, 2022.

Page, Ben. (2021). *Healing Trees, A Pocket Guide to Forest Bathing*. Cobb, CA: Mandala Publishing.

*Resources for Workplace Mental Health and Well-Being: Current Priorities of the U.S. Surgeon General*. www.hhs.gov/surgeongeneral

/priorities/workplace-well-being/resources/index.html. Accessed 18 November, 2022.

Sutton, R. (2007). *The No Asshole Rule: Building a Civilized Workplace and Surviving One That Isn't*. New York, NY: Warner Business Books.

Wikipedia contributors. "Socio-ecological system." *Wikipedia, The Free Encyclopedia*. Wikipedia, The Free Encyclopedia, 22 Nov. 2022. Web. 26 Dec. 2022.

## Chapter 3

Beck, L. & Cable, T. (2002). *Interpretation for the 21st Century: Fifteen Guiding Principles for Interpreting Nature and Culture, Second Edition*. Champaign, IL: Sagamore Publishing.

Berman, M. G., Jonides, J., & Kaplan, S. (2008). The Cognitive Benefits of Interacting with Nature. Psychological Science, 19(12), 1207–1212. https://doi.org/10.1111/j.1467-9280.2008.02225.

*Best in Show*. Directed by Christopher Guest, performances by Christopher Guest and Eugene Levy, Castle Rock Entertainment, 2000.

Brochu, L. & Merriman, T. (2015). *Personal Interpretation, Connecting Your Audience to Heritage Resources, Third Edition*. Fort Collins, CO: InterpPress.

Gilson, J. (2021). *Inspired to Inspire*. Calgary, CA: Tortuga Creative Studio.

Ham, S. (1992). *Environmental Interpretation: A Practical Guide for People with Big Ideas and Small Budgets*. Golden, CO: North American Press.

Knapp, D. (2007). *Applied Interpretation, Putting Research into Practice*. Fort Collins, CO: InterpPress.

Knudson, D., Cable, T., Beck, L. (2003). *Interpretation of Cultural and Natural Resources, Second Edition*. State College, PA: Venture Publishing Inc.

LaPage, W. "The Complete Interpreter: The Limits of Our Beliefs." *Legacy* September/October 2018, pp. 34–35.

Mazzola, N., Willey, T. "Silver Birch Cohort." Association of Nature and Forest Therapy Guides and Programs, http://www.anft.earth.

Merriman, T. Foreword. *Interpretation for the 21st Century, Fifteen Guiding Principles for Interpreting Nature and Culture, First Edition,* by Beck, L. & Cable, T. Champaign, IL: Sagamore Publishing, 2002, pp. viii–x.

Mills, E. (1923). *The Adventures of a Nature Guide.* Garden City, NY: Doubleday, Page & Co.

National Association for Interpretation, Interpretive Standards Project 2016.

Odegaard, B., Wozny, DR., Shams, L. *The effects of selective and divided attention on sensory precision and integration.* Neurosci Lett. 2016 Feb 12;614:24-8. doi: 10.1016/j.neulet.2015.12.039. Epub 2015 Dec 29. PMID: 26742638.

Risk, P. "Conducted Activities." *Interpreting the Environment, Second Edition,* by Sharpe, G. Seattle, WA: John Wiley & Sons, p. 184.

Stine, M. "Fish Hatcheries and Forest Therapy." *MAEOEgram* August 2021, pp. 6–7.

Stine, M. "Fish Hatcheries for Forest Therapy." *Michigan Forests* December 2021, pp. 24–25.

## Chapter 4

Basman C. "Special Problems, Resource Management.", 25, August 1997, Southern Illinois University, Carbondale. Class lecture.

Brochu, L., & Merriman, T. (2001). *Certified Interpretive Training Workbook.* Ft. Collins, CO: National Association for Interpretation.

Hackenmiller, S. (2019). *The Outdoor Adventurer's Guide to Forest Bathing: Using Shinrin-Yoku to Hike, Bike, Paddle, and Climb Your Way to Health and Happiness.* Lanham, MD: Falcon Guides.

Ham, S. (1992). *Environmental Interpretation: A Practical Guide for People with Big Ideas and Small Budgets.* Golden, CO: North American Press.

Ham, S. (2013). *Interpretation: Making a Difference on Purpose.* Golden, CO: Fulcrum Books.

Rowling, J.K. (1997). *Harry Potter and the Philosopher's Stone.* London: Bloomsbury Publishing.

United States. Department of Agriculture. Natural Resources Conservation Service. *Nine Steps of Conservation Planning.*

## Chapter 5

Curran, S. L., Andrykowski, M. A., & Studts, J. L. (1995). *Short Form of the Profile of Mood States (POMS-SF):* Psychometric information. *Psychological Assessment, 7*(1), 80–83. https://doi.org/10.1037/1040-3590.7.1.80. Reprinted with permission.

Photo Credits: "Wild Ride Night Bike" Parks Canada/Nicole Boutilier, Canoe "Selfie", Parks Canada/Ashley Moffat.

Wikipedia contributors. "Profile of mood states." *Wikipedia, The Free Encyclopedia.* Wikipedia, The Free Encyclopedia, 3 Feb. 2022. Web. 31 Dec. 2022.

*Photo by Heather Stine/Etched Emmet*

# ADDITIONAL SUGGESTED READINGS AND RESOURCES

## Books

Capote, T. (1980). *Music for Chameleons.* New York, NY: Vintage.

Capote, T. (2005). *The Complete Short Stories of Truman Capote.* New York, NY: Vintage Reprint.

Clifford, M.A. (2018). *Your Guide to Forest Bathing.* Newburyport, MA: Conari Press.

Greenblatt, J. (2022). *It Could Happen Here: Why America Is Tipping from Hate to the Unthinkable And How We Can Stop It.* Boston, MA: Mariner Books.

Lipman, J. (2023). *Next! The Power of Reinvention in Life and Work.* New York, NY: Mariner Books.

Mazzola, N. (2019). *Forest Bathing with Your Dog.* Middletown, DE: Blue Cloud Books.

Rikleen, L.S. (2019). *The Shield of Silence: How Power Perpetuates a Culture of Harassment and Bullying in the Workplace.* Washington, DC: American Bar Association.

Select Committee to Investigate the January 6th Attack on the United States Capitol (2022). *The January 6 Report.* New York, NY: Celadon Books.

## Forest Bathing Guides

www.amongthetrees.net
www.anft.earth
www.forestbathingfinder.com
www.nenft.com

www.natureology.me
www.toadstoolwalks.com

## Favorite Forest Bathing Props
Find small booklets, pencils, teapots, and teacups on
    www.Etsy.com and www.earthshopp.com
Find the best thermoses on earth at: www.thermos.com
Find portable campfire stoves: www.solostove.com
Find various musical instruments: www.sweetwater.com
Find multi-sensory nature exploration amazement:
    www.acornnaturalists.com

## Social Media | Websites
www.etchedemmet.com
Anti-Defamation League: www.adl.org
www.mindfulleader.org
X (Twitter): @Stopworkplacebu
www.stopworkplacebullies.com
www.pbs.org/wgbh/americanexperience/features/
    henryford-antisemitism/

## Training / Professional Development
Acorn Programs: www.acornprograms.com
Association of Nature and Forest Therapy Guides and Programs
    (ANFT): www.anft.earth
National Association for Interpretation (NAI): www.interpnet.com
National Outdoor Leadership School (NOLS): www.nols.edu/en
Strozzi Institute: www.strozziinstitute.com
World Forestry Center: www.worldforestry.org

# ACKNOWLEDGMENTS

Heartfelt gratitude to Dr. Sam Ham, Lisa Brochu, and Dr. Tim Merriman for lending their insight and expertise, providing important historical content and interpretive perspective for this book, and inspiring me to dig deeper and do my best work.

Sincere appreciation to the interpreters and forest bathing guides who graciously loaned their voices to this work: Carola Amtmann, Estelle Asselin, Dr. Cem Basman, Gwen Botting, Al Estock, Ashley Moffat, Alyse Rynor, Jill Robinson, Angel Squalls, Terri Teller, Dr. John A.Veverka, Amanda Yik.

On behalf of Non-Chosen Ones everywhere, admiration to Dr. Paul A. Moore who reminded me, *"Even nobodies are somebodies."*

A special thank you to M. Amos Clifford, founder of ANFT (www.anft.earth), international forest therapy guide and trainer, and author of *Your Guide to Forest Bathing* (2018. Newburyport, MA: Conari Press), for his gracious acquiescence supporting the content and descriptions of my training with ANFT shared in this book.

This work would not have manifested without inspiration from Nadine Mazzola and Tam Willey. They are professional guide trainers with the Association of Nature and Forest Therapy Guides and Programs (www.anft.earth) and guiding entrepreneurs. Nadine Mazzola is the author of *Forest Bathing with Your Dog* (2019. Middletown, DE: Blue Cloud Books), founder of the New England Nature & Forest Therapy Consulting (www.nenft.com), and founder of Among the Trees, Professional Development for Guides (www.amongthetrees.net). Tam Willey is the founder and guide of Toadstool Walks (www.toadstoolwalks.com). Together Tam and Nadine founded and operate Acorn Programs, a practice incorporation and development for guides (www.acornprograms.com).

Nadine and Tam taught me the language of forest bathing and evoked the innate belief of sharing kindness and reciprocity for myself, for others, and for the land. Like vessels, they held space for me which I'd long forgotten to hold for myself. And just in time.

Thank you, friends.

"*But as for me—I give them a tune on the piano every now and then just to let them know I'm cheerful.*"
—Truman Capote, *My Side of the Matter*, 1945

# ABOUT THE AUTHOR

Maureen (Mo) Stine was planted, germinated, and sprouted in the City of Chicago. Her career path began in the mid-'90s during her undergraduate years at Southern Illinois University (SIU) working summers as a recreational leader for the Chicago Park District's urban camp program and volunteering semester weekends delivering public guided interpretive hikes along the Rim Rock National Recreation Trail for the US Forest Service within the Shawnee National Forest. In 1999, Maureen received a Bachelor of Science in forestry from SIU and spent the years that followed trekking across the nation, serving nonprofit organizations and governmental agencies dedicated to park interpretation and conservation education. She launched her roving park interpreter business, Natureology, in 2009 and since then travels around the State of Michigan at will sharing her love of nature.

Authoring, developing, implementing, and evaluating environmental educational curriculum has played a pivotal role in Maureen's career. She was the co-author of the Activities Section for Michigan's Salmon in the Classroom Curriculum (2008) for the Michigan Department of Natural Resources (DNR) and was later recruited by the agency to continue a partnership with the Michigan DNR by co-authoring the Michigan School Forest Guide (2019) and authoring the hemlock woolly adelgid curriculum (2020). She later partnered with Michigan State University Extension to illustrate and co-author *Identifying Trees of Michigan* Bulletin E-2332 (2022). Maureen has authored over a dozen published essays for the National Association for Interpretation, Michigan Audubon, the Michigan Natural Resources Conservation Service's *Conservation Notes* e-newsletter, and the Michigan Alliance for Environmental and Outdoor Education.

For over two decades, Maureen has sought opportunities to expand her interpretive training to support the interpretive industry and grow better at her craft. She is a Certified Heritage Interpreter with the National Association for Interpretation, and a Certified Professional with the National Recreation and Park Association. Maureen holds facilitator certifications with national and state environmental education projects including Project W.I.L.D. (Wildlife in Learning Development), Project Learning Tree, Project W.E.T. (Water Education for Teachers), Flying Wild, and all units of the Michigan Environmental Education Curriculum Support (MEECS). She is a Certified Environmental Educator-Professional with the Michigan Alliance for Environmental and Outdoor Education (MAEOE) and was the first individual in the State of Michigan to achieve this certification on October 16, 2016.

Maureen became a certified forest therapy guide through the Association of Nature and Forest Therapy Guides and Programs in 2021. Forest bathing and instructional ice fishing for groups are her signature public programs. Maureen supports alternatives that uplift socially disadvantaged, underserved people, upholding civil rights, civil liberties, and our American perseverance of diversity, inclusion, and equal opportunity by giving voice to and promoting community networks inclusive of immigrant, refugee, and migrant, or otherwise marginalized human beings.

She spends most of her time within the Northern Lake Huron Watershed on ancestral, traditional, and contemporary Lands of the Anishnaabek—the Three Fires Confederacy of Ojibwe, Odawa, and Potawatomi peoples.

www.ingramcontent.com/pod-product-compliance
Lightning Source LLC
Chambersburg PA
CBHW052115030426
42335CB00025B/2996